Best wishes
Good luck, good health
to you and your best friend.
Bruce & Brian

Obedience Training

Obedience Training

BRUCE AND BRONWYN BARTLEY

The Crowood Press

First published in 1994 by
The Crowood Press Ltd
Ramsbury, Marlborough
Wiltshire SN8 2HR

British Library Cataloguing-in-Publication Data
A catalogue record for this book is available from the British Library.

ISBN 1 85223 799 6

DEDICATION

'TOKIE'
OB.CH.TYROCOLL BHEINN TOKEN
We were inspired by your genius and humbled by your humility.
Thank you for coming to us, though your stay was so painfully brief.

Acknowledgements
We offer our grateful thanks to Natalie and Wendy for their invaluable help and
instruction with the word processor.

Picture Credits
All photographs by Bruce Bartley
Line-drawings by Annette Findlay

Throughout this book, 'he', 'him' and 'his' have been used as neutral pronouns and
as such refer to both males and females.

Typeset by Acorn Bookwork, Salisbury, Wilts
Printed and bound in Great Britain at The Bath Press

Contents

	Preface	6
	Introduction	9
1	The Two Cornerstones of Good Obedience	17
2	Distant Control	29
3	The Stays and Temperament Test	36
4	Finishes	41
5	Heelwork Proper	47
6	The Retrieve	62
7	Class A Recall	71
8	Scent Discrimination	74
9	The Sendaway	83
10	Advanced Positions on the Move	93
11	Choosing a Puppy for Obedience	100
12	At the Show	102
	Appendices	106
	Glossary	108
	Index	112

Preface

Dogs and their training have been a major part of our lives for some thirty years since 1963 when we attended a local Road Safety club where the basic obedience of dogs in society was the main theme. It was not long, however, before a competitive spirit surfaced, along with the desire to set our skills as dog trainers and the dogs' ability to learn, against those of fellow club members. This competitive urge never detracted from the camaraderie that develops between those of a like mind, though, and we still count among our best friends some of the people we met in those early days, even if not all of them progressed – as we did – along that fascinating, rewarding, frustrating, exciting, sometimes heart-breaking, but never dull, road of competitive Obedience training. We were fortunate in those formative years to meet a gentleman named John Seal who was able to point us in the right direction by suggesting a club that was structured on more competitive lines, and a whole new world began to open up for us.

In the intervening years, through a combination of hard work, some super dogs, and help and advice from many of the best dog trainers and great characters in Obedience, we have earned a fair degree of success, attaining many hundred wins at all levels. We have enjoyed ten appearances in the Crufts Obedience Championships with four different dogs, who between them accumulated twenty-seven Obedience Certificates, two of them attaining the title 'Obedience Champion' and one of them – Ob.Ch.Tyrocoll Bheinn Token – gaining the 'Top Obedience Dog of the Year' award two years in succession in 1988 and 1989.

Not all the dogs we have owned in those thirty years have been winners at top level – a few have not won at all. Nevertheless, we can honestly say that as a result of the training they have received not one has been a social embarrassment, failed to observe the basic social niceties, or chased or worried stock. We have never been ashamed to take any of them anywhere.

In 1968 we attended a training course given by Charlie Wyant at his Littlebourne Kennels, and it is his influence that has shaped our training methods more than that of any other single individual. Such was his influence that we returned to Littlebourne in 1972 and attended every subsequent September course from then on. By 1980 we had graduated to assistant trainers, and on Charlie's retirement, in 1988, we took over ourselves. This course has now moved to a new venue, but many regulars still attend each year. We have also been invited by many training clubs nationwide to give weekend training courses, and these invitations together with judging appointments have taken us beyond the United Kingdom mainland to Holland, Belgium, Ireland, Jersey, Guernsey, and the Isle of Man.

We have been engaged as judges at all levels since the late 1960s and have judged at Championship level since 1973. In 1985 we were proud to be members of Ken Pykett's team of stewards when he judged the Crufts Obedience Championships. Being Manager and Assistant Manager of the victorious Midland Team in the inter-regional competition on that same weekend made it a very memorable occasion for us.

In all these years we have never been refused, from any of the top trainers of the day, good, honest, and well-intentioned advice on any aspect of dog training. In a fiercely competitive hobby there are very few people who will not offer help and encouragement to anyone who asks, and this is one of the principal reasons that, for us, this has always remained such a super sport.

This book, then, is our compilation of all that help, advice and instruction we have received over the years, together with a few original – we hope – additions of our own. Whether you are just contemplating a start in Obedience or are a seasoned campaigner, we sincerely hope there is something here to help you.

Introduction

Every dog should receive some degree of training. As responsible owners we owe it to our pets to ensure that they become acceptable members of society. Every dog should come when called, walk reasonably quietly on a lead, sit and wait when told, and not jump up and make a nuisance of himself. A dog that will observe these basic niceties is a joy to own; a dog that will not is an embarrassment to his owner, a nuisance to society, and is in fact being deprived of the pleasure he would derive from being accepted and admired by others.

There are many excellent dog training societies that run pet training classes with these aims in view, many in conjunction with the Kennel Club Good Citizen Scheme. The British Institute of Professional Dog Trainers also runs similar educational courses. If you are just about to embark upon your dog's basic training either of these bodies – whose addresses may be found on page 105 – will be happy to provide local contacts for suitable training societies.

If by now you have already attended one of these courses with any degree of success, you may have stumbled across the theme of this book in your approach to your dog's training; what we call the three 'Ts'. These are Temperament, Tone of voice, and Timing.

A few people are naturally good animal trainers. This comes from an almost subconscious ability to time their commands, praise, even reprimands to match the dog's response. This is accompanied by a contrast in tone of voice to reinforce their words. However, you do not have to be an absolute 'natural' to train a dog successfully; by careful observation of the three Ts, almost anyone can improve the standards of his handling and his dog's training.

So what is the point of improving beyond the basic social requirements? The answer to that question lies in human nature itself. The human animal is by and large a competitive one. Sometimes at work, but certainly at sport and leisure, the competitive urge is never far from the surface. In our relationship with our dogs these tendencies reveal themselves in many ways. Is my dog a better specimen of the breed? Will my dog guard or track better than the next? Can my dog herd sheep better than that? Can my dog flush or retrieve game more efficiently than his dog? Can my dog jump higher or faster? Is my dog more obedient than others?

All these questions can be addressed in the wide variety of canine competition open to us: Breed Shows, Working Trials, Sheep Dog Trials, Field Trials, Agility, and Obedience Competitions. Of these, Obedience is arguably – from a numerical point of view – the most popular, and certainly it is the most accessible. Entries at Obedience shows are the most numerous, the necessary equipment is nominal, and because it is not too demanding physically it is open to the widest range of age and mobility.

What is Competitive Obedience?

Briefly, Obedience competitions consist of a regulated and specified sequence of manoeuvres, carried out in turn by a group of people with their dogs, under the direction and scrutiny of a judge who is appointed to decide which dog and handler complete the tests with the least deviation from the standards outlined in the competition rules. In the execution of these manoeuvres an immediate and obedient response from the dog to all his handler's commands is a prerequisite, but the curriculum of exercises and the way in which they are required to be executed goes much further than this. The dog is not just required to obey commands but is also judged on the accuracy and precision with which he responds. Furthermore, after progressing beyond the two junior classes of competition – Beginners and Novice – help from the handler in the form of more than one command in order to complete an exercise carries a penalty in the form of marks deducted.

It is, in fact, the precision and consequent elegance with which the dogs are required to work that sets this branch of canine competition apart from the others for us; the term 'Obedience' is barely adequate, for what has evolved is more akin to the Dressage Competition of the equine world.

There are four basic levels of complexity of Obedience test in the United Kingdom, although there are six levels of graduation. This is because at the lower end of the scale there are two classes (Beginner and Novice) that have the same content.

The term 'Beginner' applies to both dog and handler. This class is restricted not only to dogs that have not won more than two Beginner classes or one other, but similarly to handlers. In this way the real newcomers have a chance to compete against one another without the pressure of facing more experienced competitors. The Novice class, although the content and complexity is the same as in Beginners, is open to all competitors – experienced or not – and the entry restriction is only based on the wins accrued by the dog. Once you, as a handler, have won two Beginners classes, you will never again be eligible, whereas each young dog you acquire will commence his Obedience career in Novice. There, you will find yourself competing against people with all levels of experience.

At the other end of the scale, the most advanced class is Class C. Here also there are two divisions, each having the same basic content. Open Class C is open to all, although your dog should have progressed upward to this level by winning the prescribed maximum number of lower classes. Your dog must have progressed through a series of first places through the lower classes and gained a win plus three other places in Open Class C before being eligible to compete in Championship C. There are about forty shows during the year countrywide which carry Championship status.

A win in Championship C dog or bitch class at one of these shows automatically qualifies dog and handler for the forthcoming Obedience Championships at Crufts. On attaining three Championship wins, the dog becomes an Obedience Champion. This is the highest honour that can be achieved.

In between, the graduation from Beginner/ Novice to Class C is through Classes A and B. Obviously, the complexity and degree of difficulty of each test increases as one progresses.

In addition to Open and Championship, there are three other classifications of show: Limit, Sanction, and Exemption – each of which can be of value as an introduction to the show environment without, perhaps, carrying the same prestige and accompanying pressure.

All British Obedience Shows are run under the auspices of the Kennel Club and dogs must be registered to enable them to compete. A full description of each test and each exercise therein, together with the marking allocation and qualifying requirements and restrictions, is contained in the Kennel Club Rules and Regulations, section G. All pedigree dogs will be dual registered so that they may be entered in Breed Shows as well. However, you do not have to own a pedigree dog to compete, as the Obedience and Working Trials Register is open to all dogs including cross-breeds; indeed, over the years there have been several cross-breeds competing very successfully, many gaining their Obedience Champion title, and at least two having won Crufts.

If all this appeals to you as a progression from basic training, the society or club you have been attending may well also cater for competitive work as well. If not, the Kennel Club will be happy to provide local contacts for competitive training clubs.

There are many other countries worldwide where similar though individual forms of Obedience competition have evolved. By necessity this book is structured around English Kennel Club rules, and it should be noted that there must be many finer points which vary from country to country. We believe, however, that our philosophy of simple step-by-step build-up in the teaching of all exercises, combined with the correct application of aids to ensure that the dog is never allowed to go wrong, can be adopted wherever dog trainers compete throughout the world.

The Three Ts

We believe that effective competitive training must centre on what we like to call the three 'Ts': Temperament, Tone of voice and Timing.

Temperament

To begin with the handler must consider his own temperament as well as the dog's, and he must continue this self-analysis throughout his training career, particularly when he acquires a new dog, for each one is different; dogs are as individual as humans.

If you are a strong assertive personality, it will be easy for you – without realizing – to flatten and subdue a dog whose temperament is perhaps not as robust as you expect it to be. It is very easy to put too much pressure on your dog through your own desire to succeed. Over-training, and more especially over-correction, can upset many dogs every bit as much as harsh physical handling. We see very few instances of intentional cruelty in Obedience, but from time to time we do see dogs being subjected to unnecessary stress through over-training or because they have been corrected for mistakes that are largely the fault of their handler's poor training methods. You may have to step back from time to time and ask yourself, 'Am I putting too much mental pressure on my dog?'

Conversely, if you are of a quieter disposition and you have a dog of more flamboyant character, it often happens that the dog tries to become the more dominant member of the partnership. Dogs are, after all, pack animals, and if a clearly discernible pack leader is not perceived, the temptation for a more dominant type of dog to take on this role becomes irresistible. In your day-to-day contact with your dog, from the earliest puppy days, you must constantly ensure that you do not let your heart rule your head. Remember a good saying: 'I am kind, but I rule'.

It is vital that handler and dog are able to form a bond based not just on love but mutual respect. As the provider of food, security, comfort, and health care, you are entitled to the role of pack leader and the respect that goes with it, and you should demand it – not of course by resorting to physical violence at every turn, but by judicious matching of *your* temperament with that of the *dog* so that he fully understands when you are pleased or cross without becoming either cowed or taking advantage of you.

On the other hand, you must also respect the dog's qualities, which are far superior to ours: sense of smell particularly, and often hearing and sight. Depending on the breed, dogs can also be faster across the ground and stronger than humans. We should be able to draw pleasure from these qualities rather than seeking to suppress or override them.

Tone of Voice

In your working relationship with your dog, his desire to please you must be paramount. We often say that the greatest titbit available to your dog should be what comes out of your mouth. This accounts for the second 'T': tone of voice.

If you are genuinely pleased with your dog and your praise comes from the heart, your dog will sense it. You must learn to be as uninhibited as possible, and you should not be afraid of your voice pitch making you sound silly to other people. This is one of the reasons why women generally make better handlers than men, who find it more difficult to 'let go'.

On the other hand, if your dog incurs your displeasure, that should be equally obvious from your tone of voice. Contrast between praise and correction is necessary for the dog to appreciate the praise fully. Correction should rarely come during competition training but rather only when real naughtiness, defiance, or aggression is apparent, such as a tendency to fight other dogs, attack humans, behave destructively, or show signs of any other serious vices.

Tone of voice is also extremely useful for reinforcing specific commands. For instance, the use of the dog's name in three totally different tones of voice, preceding the commands 'Sit', 'Down', and 'Stand', together with clear enunciation of the vowel sounds in those three words, can consolidate considerably the consistency of the dog's response in the Distance Control exercise or on the Advanced Positions on the move in Heelwork. An excited 'Where is it' or 'Find it' when setting your dog up for Scent can well stimulate him to do just that. (There will be more about tone of voice for commands as we cover the various exercises.)

Timing

Perhaps the most fundamental 'T' of all is timing. A dog will work happily and confidently if he is used to receiving the correct signals from his handler in the form of consistent deportment and commands *in time* for him to respond. Sloppy deportment and late commands are the largest contributing factors in creating a dull, miserable, and unresponsive dog. Ironically, it is usually this type of hand-

ler that one hears complaining that the content of a particular test is not stimulating enough and is causing boredom in his dog.

It is absolutely vital that your commands and any other aids you apply are given in such a way as to allow the dog time to assimilate and respond to them. This applies particularly to the young dog learning his trade and in Beginners and Novice competition. Remember – say it; do it. In other words, give the command, then apply whatever aid is necessary, then complete the manoeuvre.

The greatest reason why all the top trainers can bring out a young dog into Novice, and within a matter of weeks have collected two or more wins and be on their way up the ladder, is because of the way they time their commands.

Simplification of the Exercises

In the ensuing chapters we will be considering the various exercises that combine to make up each level of competition – broadly in the order which we would set about teaching a young pup, although not strictly in the order in which you will require them as you ascend through the classes. However, there are a few more general points we would like to cover before we leave this introductory chapter.

At the commencement of training you will see that we attempt to break up all the exercises into small easily assimilated parts, only combining the whole when we are sure that the dog is fully confident in what is required of him. All our training methods are designed to ensure as much as possible that the dog cannot go wrong. Thus, on completion of a manoeuvre, all that remains to be done is to praise the dog for being correct. Training by default – that is to say allowing faults to occur and then correcting them – is definitely out. If your dog does make a mistake, it is as a result of your training methods. Ignore the faults, and go back and start again applying the correct aids to ensure that the error is not repeated. The dog must not be allowed to become confused and apprehensive by being constantly told that something is wrong.

You should learn to mix work and play at a ratio of at least five to one, i.e. for every minute you spend training your dog, you should spend at least five playing with him. If he will not play and respond to praise, he will not work – at least not to his full potential.

Your dog's vocabulary will increase as his training advances, but it will never be very extensive, so ensure that commands are kept simple. Never use two or more words where one will do; never use multi-syllabic words where single will do. Your dog must of course recognize his name, particularly as a recall command, although beware of using it too much in front of certain other commands.

Before even the most elementary competition exercises can be commenced, the dog must understand and respond immediately to the 'Sit' and 'Down' commands. We assume that these will have been taught and be well established at basic training level, but if you wish to reinforce either of these responses, *see* chapters 1, 2, and 10. It is essential that an immediate response to both commands is established before proceeding further, particularly the 'Down', which, Obedience apart, could save your dog's life.

A common mistake that many trainers make is not saying 'Down' firmly enough for fear of the dog thinking that he is being chastised. They try to say the command both firmly and quietly, and the sound comes out as a sort of strangled squawk, which the dog finds difficult to respond to anyway. The command should be given firmly and clearly, making full use of the vowel sound and followed by plenty of genuine praise when the dog has responded. The dog will soon understand that a firm Down command is not a chastisement.

Equipment

As a conclusion to this chapter, we would like to offer a few words of advice regarding equipment. Although as we have already said, the amount of equipment required for Obedience is fairly nominal, it is important to get it right. Apart from tone of voice, your main contact with your dog is through the lead and collar, and you should feel comfortable about both.

Some people say that only a leather lead will do, but there are now many excellent substitutes on the market, made from woven rope or nylon, and it is worth getting a feel for all these mediums. In the end, you should pick that with which you are most comfortable, but whatever you decide upon it should be flexible enough to fold and loop easily and light enough to transfer quickly to either hand. At the collar end, the buckle should be as small as possible and smooth and safe to operate quickly. At your end it should have a loop and a steel ring so that its length of 3–3½ft (90–

Sit at heel. Give the command 'Sit', at the same time bringing the lead up and your left hand down on to the dog's quarters.

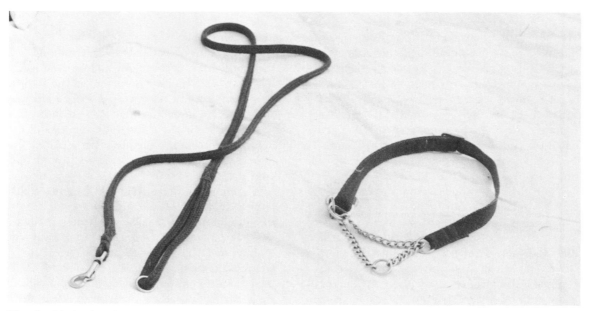

Neat buckle lead and half-slip collar.

105cm) can be extended by clipping on a second lead if required (*see* chap. 7). Remember that your lead is a tool, and as such it should be chosen, cared for, and used with the same consideration any craftsman shows his equipment. You should eventually be able to transfer it from hand to hand, raise it, lower it, tighten it, loosen it, etc. with the dexterity of a master craftsman.

Some people are not entirely happy with metal slip-chain collars, but as long as they are not abused they are in no way unkind to the dog. The traditional leather buckle collar, however, is also unsuitable for training. If too loose, it can easily be pulled off; if tight enough to prevent this occurring, it may not be comfortable for the dog.

A happy medium is the half-slip collar made from nylon webbing and steel links. This collar can open and close like a check-chain, but can be adjusted so that when it is fully tightened it still can not induce more than a light pressure around the dog's neck. Nevertheless, the sound of the metal links can still 'talk' to the dog. All our dogs are trained in these collars.

All the Obedience tests include a retrieve exercise, and in Beginners, Novice, and Class A the retrieve article is the handler's own dumbbell. Many people make their own but very few of these D.I.Y. jobs stand the test of time. The size of the dumb-bell depends somewhat on the size of your dog, but you should avoid very small ones as even a small dog is capable of retrieving relatively large articles, and a very small bell is easily lost in long grass. At the other end of the scale, a very large bell can be very cumbersome for you to carry around, and large breeds do not necessarily need a 'macho' sized dumb-bell to match. One no more than 7in (18cm) long by 4in (10cm) across is plenty high enough.

It is worth investing in one of the quality bells available from the many stalls at dog shows. These can be made from nylon or turned out of a whole piece of wood. Many bright colours are available but not necessarily effective. Black and white are the colours most easily distinguished by the dog.

Other odds and ends, such as practice retrieve articles and sendaway markers, will be collected and carried about in your car as your experience progresses.

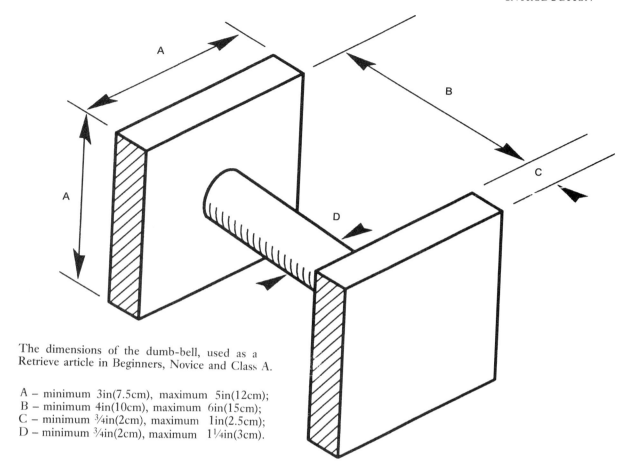

The dimensions of the dumb-bell, used as a Retrieve article in Beginners, Novice and Class A.

A – minimum 3in(7.5cm), maximum 5in(12cm);
B – minimum 4in(10cm), maximum 6in(15cm);
C – minimum ¾in(2cm), maximum 1in(2.5cm);
D – minimum ¾in(2cm), maximum 1¼in(3cm).

Finally, here are some suggestions on clothing, beginning with footwear. Common sense dictates that shoes should be comfortable, with rubber soles that can grip on grass and other surfaces (there are still a few indoor shows on relatively smooth surfaces). However, very light trainers or pumps do not necessarily help in placing your feet accurately and keeping your balance. A more substantial leather shoe with a soft rubber sole can be much easier to 'control'. It will also be more resistant to wet grass.

On the subject of wet grass and the weather that creates it, a light waterproof suit and a pair of wellington boots are essential to avoid a soaking, as these days most shows are outdoors, and judging has to continue – rain or shine. It is worth while spending some time working your dog in this more cumbersome attire to get him used to you being in it. Otherwise, clothing should just be smart and comfortable. Avoid long coats or anything that will flap and distract the dog. Never work with your coat or bodywarmer undone.

15

Key

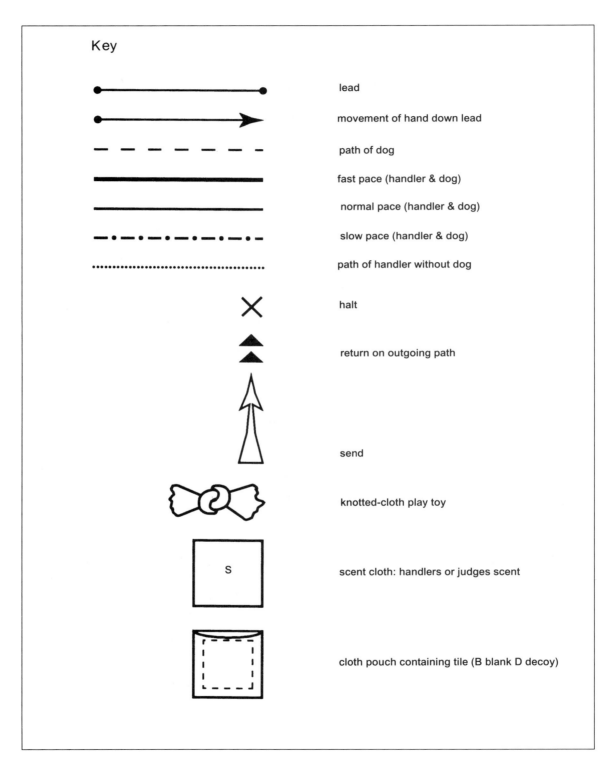

lead

movement of hand down lead

path of dog

fast pace (handler & dog)

normal pace (handler & dog)

slow pace (handler & dog)

path of handler without dog

halt

return on outgoing path

send

knotted-cloth play toy

scent cloth: handlers or judges scent

cloth pouch containing tile (B blank D decoy)

CHAPTER 1

The Two Cornerstones of Good Obedience

There are two cornerstones which should form the foundation of all your future work with your dog: an accurate Novice Recall and undivided attention in Heelwork. This chapter is devoted to the more informal, repetitive, but most of all relaxed and fun ways in which these can be acquired.

Novice Recall

Novice Recall is not just an exercise to complete correctly in this, the junior of classes; it goes much deeper. If you do not have a consistent and precise Novice Recall you will not have a reliable Retrieve, Scent, Distance Control, or even Sendaway. In short, it is the basis of all the set-piece exercises, and for that reason we will dwell on this aspect of training. Indeed, we will continue to revert back to it throughout training and play.

Basics to Remember
- Ensure your dog is sitting straight and comfortably by your side to begin.
- Command your dog to 'Sit' or 'Wait' i.e. reserve the command 'Stay' for the stays exercise.
- Leave your dog by stepping off with your right foot. (Step off with your left foot when commencing Heelwork.)
- Ensure full attention from your dog whilst walking away.
- On instruction to Halt and About-turn, turn and place your feet correctly, but keep your hands behind you or at your sides until instructed to call.
- On instruction to call your dog, use his name once in a bright commanding tone and complete your Recall position with your hands in front of you.
- Say 'Sit' early, i.e. when your dog is still approximately 1½–2yd (1.4–1.8m) from you.

The Exercise

Commence with your dog in the Sit on your left-hand side. On the steward's command tell your dog to wait (there are no last commands in Novice, so further commands may be given when leaving the dog). Leave your dog. At approximately twenty paces halt, turn, and face your dog. On the steward's command call your dog to the Present position in the Sit in front of you. On the steward's command, Finish your dog to heel. On the steward's command 'Exercise finished', release your dog for praise.

Typical faults likely to incur penalty points are inattention requiring a repeat command to Come, slow Recall, crooked Sit on Present, off-centre Present, backward Sit, Present too close, wide Finish, slow Finish, crooked Sit on Finish, and backward or forward Sit on Finish.

Teaching the Exercise

As in every aspect of training, the exercise should be broken down into small easy-to-learn segments.

Novice Recall – Step One

Command 'Sit'. Leave on your right foot, maintaining the dog's position with the lead.

Turn to face the dog.

Step One

Teaching Novice Recall commences with the dog sitting at heel on the lead. With the end of the lead in your right hand and passing over your left hand held palm upward, tell your dog to 'Sit', or 'Wait'. Leave your dog, stepping off with the right foot (you do not have to go very far). Ensure that the dog maintains his position with light upward pressure on the lead, using the left hand. Turn and face your dog, continuing with the occasional 'Wait' command. Ensure that your dog's full attention remains on you; the split second he glances away, say 'Watch me' in an urgent tone and make a very slight upward movement with the left hand. After a few seconds, return to the Present position in front of your dog, ensuring that you are in line with a straight Sit. You can now praise your

dog for being correct, and he hasn't even moved yet.

Step Two

The next step, which is probably the most important phase of instruction, is what we call the 'Come fore' recall. Set off with your dog on the lead. (You are not doing Heelwork for this can be a fun manoeuvre carried out dozens of times while out for a walk with your dog.) After a few paces, say your dog's name in a bright commanding tone as you begin to pace backward, adopting the Recall position with your hands as you go. As your dog turns to face and follow you, shorten the lead, wait until you judge him to be straight, and give the command 'Sit' while still moving backward. It is important that the dog is encouraged to begin to sit while

Maintain the Sit while facing the dog at lead's length.

Approach dog to finish in the straight Present position. Praise.

there is still some forward movement. In this way there is a much better chance that the Sit will be straight. If you wait until you have both stopped moving, the dog will tend to 'flop' to one side or the other, so get your command in early, a pace before you come to a halt. This is your first chance to capitalize on the skill of good timing. It is essential to be able to judge when the time is right to Sit your dog without resorting to correction.

Step Three

For the third and last stage before putting the whole exercise together, command and leave your dog on the lead as in Step One. After a few seconds' wait, ensuring attention at all time, instead of returning to your dog, call him, using his name in a bright tone and adopting the Recall position. As your dog begins to move, take a few paces backward and say 'Sit' when you judge that he is straight but still on the move. Halt just as he sits, but if you perceive a crooked sit – even at the last second – take another pace or two and try again. Always try to ensure the correct result without having to correct the dog. Then all that is left is to praise him for being right.

The three phases can be taught simultaneously, and when the 'Come fore' recall is perfected it should be possible for you to adopt the Recall position wherever your dog is, and as soon as he sees you his natural reaction should be to come to you and sit in the Present position. When you have achieved this, you are well on the road to a reliable and consistent Retrieve and – even more important in later training – Scent.

19

Novice Recall – Step Two

Walk forward with dog, setting off on your left foot.

Call dog, using his name, in a bright tone. Walk backwards, at the same time using the Novice Recall sign.

Novice Recall – Step Three

Give the command 'Sit'. Leave dog, and turn to face him, as in Novice Recall, stage one.

Call dog's name in Recall tone. Pace backwards in Novice Recall position.

While moving backwards, give the command 'Sit'.

If dog sits straight, halt, and then praise. If not, continue to walk backwards repeating the 'Sit' command until he does sit straight. Timing is important here: try to give the command when you can see that the dog will probably sit straight. In this way you give him the best chance of getting it right first time.

Give the 'Sit' command when you judge the dog to be straight.

In this exercise repetition is important but it need not be boring. Remember your three Ts; no training should be a chore for either of you and with the correct timing to ensure accuracy, genuine and excited praise when you get it right, the whole procedure can be repeated again and again while still remaining fun for both of you.

Novice Recall – Finished Stage

Remove lead. Give the command 'Sit'. Leave the dog, setting off on your right foot.

Turn and face the dog, keeping your hands still and out of the way until you are ready to recall. Continue to command 'Wait' or 'Sit' if necessary.

The Complete Exercise

When you feel confident that your dog has assimilated the three preliminary stages, it is time to try to combine them, but don't try to rush it.

With your dog at the Sit, take the lead off and give the command to 'Sit' or 'Wait'. Leave your dog, but only go two or three paces before turning to face him, repeating the command as necessary before calling him using name and Recall sign *only*. Pace back, and say 'Sit' early as before. Only gradually increase the distance each time. If your dog anticipates, go back and start again; do not chastise him if he comes before he is called.

When you are able to leave your dog for the full distance, remember to call him once using his name in a bright commanding tone and adopt the Recall position. Avoid further encouragement until your dog has reached you and sat correctly in the Present position, at which time you can break the exercise and praise him generously; in this way you will cultivate a speedy Return to you for this is where your dog can count on a reward. Too much encouragement on the way will dilute the pleasure on arrival and can lead to a slow Return.

Now you will have a consistent, accurate, and happy Novice Recall, but don't forget that constant reversion to this exercise throughout your dog's life – particularly the 'Come fore' – long after you have ceased to need it in the competition ring, is important to maintain

Call your dog, using his name only, while at the same time adopting the Novice Recall position.

Just before the dog reaches you, give the command 'Sit'.

quick Returns and accurate Presents in Retrieve and Scent.

You will notice that we have not covered the Finish – that is the Return to the heel position from the Present – in this section. This is because we teach and practise it as a separate exercise, and we shall therefore deal with it in a separate chapter (*see* chap. 4).

There are two reasons for this. Firstly, if you always complete your Novice Recall, or Retrieve, or Scent, with the Finish, your dog will develop the tendency to anticipate or to Present with a bias in the direction he expects to Finish (right or left). Secondly, if your dog has completed a good Recall, Retrieve, or Scent with a good Present in training, we prefer to praise at that point rather than dilute the value

of the praise by waiting until the Finish has been completed. We very rarely, in training, complete an exercise by Finishing from the Present.

Problems and Solutions

Anticipation

'Anticipation' is when the dog will not wait until being called before coming to the handler. This is usually caused by nothing more than the desire to rejoin you. The fault develops because you haven't the heart to curb this very pleasing trait, and why should you? Anticipation is always regarded as a 'good' fault and is

23

much more easily cured than reluctance, laziness, or truculence.

To cure the problem, simply return to your dog (Present position) after a few paces, then ten or fifteen paces, without calling at all. After all, the Recall itself is no problem for you. Practise the 'Wait' part, and praise if correct. The actual 'Come' and straight Present can be practised in the fun 'Come fore' sessions outlined earlier.

Slow Recalls

'Slow recall' is when the dog walks in with little or no enthusiasm. This is often caused by too much encouragement on the way in, or by correcting inaccurate Presents rather than not letting them happen in the first place.

Try leaving your dog at fast pace and calling immediately on turning to face. You could even try turning away and running on after your Recall command, but ensure that you turn to face your dog and back away as per 'Come fore' recall before he catches up with you.

Attentive Heelwork

The other fundamental cornerstone of consistent competitive Obedience is undivided attention from your dog in Heelwork. There will be more about the exercise itself in chapter 5; for the moment, we are concerned only with maintaining the dog's attention while he is accompanying you in a forward direction. The dog must also maintain a constant position, with his shoulder level with his handler's leg. Deviation from this position, forward, backward, or sideways, will result in loss of marks during competition.

You should begin by walking at a slow/medium pace with the dog in a left-hand circle so that the added complication of turns does not break the pattern until it is firmly established in the dog's mind. During this learning stage, the exercise is carried out exclusively on the lead, which should be held in the right

hand, nearly tight, over the left-hand side of the body. The left hand just rests on the lead, lower down, and is used merely to offer light restraint backward or gentle encouragement forward – whichever is necessary to maintain the correct position.

In this position any movement of either hand is directly above the dog's head and will encourage him to look directly upward. If the right hand is further across the right-hand side of your body, any movement will encourage your dog to look across you with a consequent tendency for the hindquarters to swing out into a position known appropriately enough as 'crabbing'. This is regarded as a fault by most judges and will result in marks being deducted.

The Playtoy

The inclusion of a playtoy to heighten your dog's interest, particularly in the formative weeks, is an excellent idea. If it is in the form of a knotted cloth, this can also be adapted for teaching Scent. The toy should be held in the right hand together with the lead.

The term 'playtoy' should be carefully defined and understood. A young dog will have several 'toys' with which he is left to play as he grows up – old slippers and shoes, dog chews, etc., but your mutual 'playtoy' will have a special significance. It will be the toy with which you play together, the link that brings you close and gradually forms the bond which eventually transcends any material or tangible item. This is the toy that you throw for him and chase after on hands and knees together, and play tug-of-war with. No wonder it should form such a vital part of Heelwork attention training.

Attention should be taught, initially, with the dog in the Sit position at your side. With the lead held as described, the playtoy can be agitated slightly accompanied with the command 'Watch me'. If the dog complies he should be praised profusely.

When undivided attention has been achieved on the spot, try taking a few paces together.

Play time for Tally and Teigha with knotted cloth playtoy.

Before starting off, use your dog's name, followed by the command 'Heel', and step off with the left foot. If the attention can be maintained for even two or three paces, break off, praise, and play vigorously. Set up again, and after moving off try to maintain the attention for a few paces more before breaking off and praising again.

As more and more consistent attention is achieved, Halts (Sit at heel) can be introduced. As in Novice Recall, the timing of the commands is all-important as the desired effect is to promote the commencement of the Sit while there is still some forward impulsion in your dog. There are three aids: one verbal and two physical. Give the command 'Sit' (don't waste time by saying your dog's name in front of this command) and a split second later apply the

two physical aids – up with the right hand applying light upward tension on the lead, and down with the left hand applying firm (but not a slap) downward and inward pressure into the dog's flank. Do not release these aids until the dog has fully responded and is firmly settled in the Sit position. A weak and sloppy application of these aids will only result in the dog settling against your hand into a crooked Sit.

It is not necessary to start from the Halt every time. Try to walk back into 'Heelwork mode' from play sometimes. If your dog does not look up at you for very long to begin with, try to avoid the temptation to manipulate his head into the desired position with your hands. Too much hand contact of this kind will be irritating to the dog and is more likely to result in a stubborn refusal to watch at all. It is far

Attention on the spot with and without playtoy. Note that both hands are positioned on the left side of the body.

better to encourage with your voice and wait patiently for the head to come up even for a brief moment and praise vigorously when it does. This is where timing is important again. You must be ready to praise as soon as the attention becomes apparent and not find yourself praising too late when the attention has been lost again.

Watch Me

There is no specific requirement in the rules that the dog should watch his handler, but it is broadly recognized that 100 per cent attention can not be achieved without this attitude and the 'proof of the pudding is in the eating', for there are simply no longer any top-winning dogs who do not watch.

Using the foregoing methods, it should soon be possible for you to walk with your dog in a left-hand circle without him taking his eyes off you for a second, while with correct use of tone of voice in praise it remains a fun exercise. Not until you have achieved this should you consider introducing turns. In the meantime, of course, you can be considering how to introduce turns through your own correct deportment, *without* your dog.

Heelwork Mode

When you are confident that you have achieved 100 per cent attention holding the lead in both hands as described, you may feel more comfortable adopting a slightly more natural posture while walking in Heelwork. The lead may be

Heelwork attention in left-hand circle. Tally, Tarka, and Teigha all know their place.

held in the left hand only, looped so that it is nearly, but not quite, tight while training but allowed to hang a little looser when working in the ring so that you do not have a 'tight lead'. In order to ensure that the lead remains still and at a constant length, the left arm should not be swung so the left hand should be kept close to your side approximately waist- or top-of-leg level. You may feel more comfortable now in allowing your right arm to swing naturally as a balancing (smartening) action, i.e. left foot, right arm forward together. Carefully controlled, without being exaggerated, this natural action can be an aid to deportment, boosting confidence and transmitting information to the dog without being – or being interpreted as – an extra command.

You must also be able to develop the skill of looking mainly straight ahead while being aware of where your dog is and what he is doing. The resulting one arm still, one arm swinging, head set slightly to one side, are generally recognized as what we call 'Heelwork mode'. It must not be too exaggerated of course, as this can lead to an unnatural-looking posture often known as 'Collie cramp'.

Having graduated to a natural posture for Heelwork, you should still be able to revert to the original more instructional handling and use of the lead when progressing through the various turns, changes of pace and later teaching positions on the move and whenever any minor faults recur and require tidying up.

CHAPTER 2

Distant Control

Distant control is considered to be an advanced exercise, so one might question whether it should be introduced at this early stage. We feel it should – for three reasons.

Firstly, our work so far has been largely informal, with (in the Novice Recall) the vast majority of the time spent doing 'Come fore' recalls as a fun exercise while out for walks, and (in the elementary Heelwork) breaking regularly into vigorous play. Commencement of the Distant Control exercise can begin to introduce, without any pressure, a little quiet discipline.

Secondly, taught thoroughly and correctly, the exercise can take a considerable time to become established firmly in the dog's mind – several months, perhaps even a year. It is, therefore, better to teach it in leisurely easy stages than to have to rush it later when you may suddenly find yourself rapidly approaching the time when you will need it in the ring.

Thirdly, for Beginners/Novice handlers, it helps to provide motivation and ambition to reach further than the immediate limits of the lower classes.

The Exercise

The handler is required to set the dog up in either the Down, Sit, or Stand position. On 'Last command' from the steward, the handler may speak once to the dog to tell him to wait, then with an instruction from the steward the handler walks some twenty paces and is told to halt and face the dog. The dog is then required, on command from his handler when instructed by the steward, to take up six com-binations of the Sit, Stand or Down positions. The combination is the same for every dog in any particular class but varies from show to show. Commands from the handler may comprise the dog's name, followed by a vocal command (one word) or the dog's name followed by a signal (an arm or leg movement). Our own preference is a vocal command as variation in tone of voice can provide confidence-boosting reinforcement.

Penalty points are incurred if the dog does not respond immediately, and a missed position requiring an extra command is quite heavily penalized. You may also find that an unconscious head or body movement accompanying your command is marked down. In addition, if the dog makes more than a body-length in any direction (usually, but not always, forward) in the execution of the six positions, points will be deducted. It is quite a demanding test, and perhaps you begin to see why it is best started early.

Teaching the Exercise

Breaking the exercise down into small easily assimilated sections is more important here than anywhere; again we start with the dog on the lead.

Sit to Down and Back

It is best to teach one sequence at a time and not progress to the next until the first is firmly established in the dog's brain. We start with the Sit to Down and the Down back to Sit.

Begin with the dog in the Sit position by

your side; have the end of the lead in your right hand, and let it pass over your left hand, palm upward. As a Wait command, in order to differentiate between this exercise and others, such as Recall or Retrieve, we give the command 'Control'. Then step off with the right foot using the left hand under the lead over the dog's neck to ensure that he remains in the Sit position. Take just one pace and stand semi-facing your dog. Gently release the lead from your left hand and let it loop to within about 9–10in (22–25cm) of the ground, still held in the right hand. Give the command 'Down' (you may precede the command with your dog's name if you wish, but ensure it is said in a firm deep tone to match the 'Down' sound). As soon as you have given the command (but not before), apply the aid, which is to put your

left foot on the lead and take it firmly but smoothly down. Ensure that your right hand does not also follow down, negating the effect. It is important that only one command is given and the aid is applied correctly and maintained until the dog is in the Down.

Immediately the dog has completely responded, praise vigorously with voice only and keep your foot on the lead to make sure the dog does not jump up. After a few seconds the second half of the first sequence – Down to the Sit – can be attempted.

Transfer the weight of your body from the right foot on to the left, take up the slack of the lead with the open palm of your left hand, and give the 'Sit' command. (Again if you wish to precede the command with your dog's name you may do so. This time say it in a crisp

Sit to Down to Sit

From Sit to the Down.

From the Down to the Sit.

medium tone to match the sound of the 'Sit' command.) Immediately after you have given the 'Sit' command, apply the aid, which is a gentle upward and backward tightening of the lead by raising the left hand accompanied by a sliding of the right foot along the ground to touch your dog's front paws. Do not snatch the lead or tap the dog's toes with your feet. All movements should be smooth and firmly gentle.

After going through the foregoing sequences several times, using the aids described, starting at the Sit, give your command without fully applying the aid (just lift your left foot slightly without putting it on the lead). If the dog responds, praise quietly with voice only; if he doesn't, complete the manoeuvre of applying the aid without further command, and try a few more times. Similarly, from the Down, try the command followed by a slightly less obvious aid. When the dog will obey the Down

from the Sit command and the Sit from the Down command without the use of any aids, the next sequence can be started. This will be from the Sit to the Stand and from the Stand back to the Sit.

Sit to Stand and Back

Again from the Sit, on the lead, following the command 'Control', leave and stand semi-facing your dog with the end of the lead in the right hand passing over the left hand, palm upward. With the weight of your body on the right foot, give your Stand command. This is the one position where it is generally regarded that the dog's name *should* precede the command, and it *should* be in a bright, slightly extended tone similar to that used for Recall. You may think that this has the effect of causing the dog to come forward, but if the accompanying aids are used consistently, and the dog

Sit to Stand to Sit

To Stand from the Sit.

To Sit from the Stand.

is made aware – with the initial 'Control' command – of the particular exercise in which he is engaged, an on-the-spot reaction will not take long to establish. Immediately you have given the command, apply the aid, which consists of the maintenance of slight upward and backward pressure from the lead, accompanied by a sliding of your left foot gently along the floor under your dog's tummy to make contact with the back legs. If applied correctly, it should not be necessary to use your left foot to lift the dog into the Stand. Indeed, this should be avoided, for if you need to resort to this, it is you who is carrying out the exercise rather than the dog. Give the command once, and maintain the aid until the dog responds.

Many dogs will respond initially into the Stand, move away clockwise, and drop back into the Sit. If this happens, start the exercise with your dog parallel and close to a wall, so that he can not move away from you. Quiet praise upon correct response while maintaining the aid is again required.

To return your dog from the Stand to the Sit, transfer the weight of your body onto your left foot and give your Sit command immediately followed by the aid – exert slight backward pressure with the lead and slide your right foot up to your dog's toes. In this way the dog will sit backward instead of scooping into the position which creates slight forward movement.

Following several of these combinations using the aids described, try them with the aids becoming less and less pronounced until you have the Sit to Stand and Stand to Sit on command only.

Down to Stand and Back

The remaining combination – Stand to Down and Down to Stand – is obviously the most difficult and requires a combination of the aids previously described, particularly the Stand from Down. Begin with the dog in the Sit position, and apply the Down command as

Down to Stand

From the Down, calling the dog's name.

To the Stand, giving the command 'Stand'.

Down to Stand – Alternative Method

To Down from the Stand, using the alternative method of placing the foot on the lead.

previously described. You should then be in position with the end of the lead in your right hand and the weight of your body on the right foot. Do not forget the Stand command should be preceded with the dog's name. As you say your dog's name, transfer the weight of your body onto your left foot, use your left hand to create light upward and backward lead pressure, and apply the Sit aid by sliding your right foot up to the dog's front paws, but in one smooth movement as the dog's name is followed by the Stand command, transfer the weight of your body back onto the right foot and apply the Stand aid, sliding your left foot along the ground under the dog's tummy to touch the back legs, all the time maintaining the slight backward pressure with the left hand on the lead.

It is important that the Stand through the Sit is achieved with one flowing movement of the aids, so that the dog does not dwell in the Sit position. This could cost marks if it is too pronounced in the ring.

From the Stand back to the Down, the same aid as for Sit to Down can be applied. However, some backward bias can be encouraged by (having given the Down command) placing your hands on the point of shoulder and pressing gently but firmly downward and backward. This is the only time we advise contact with the dog in training for the exercise, but it is worth it just for this one position to form the habit of slight backward movement. Again this combination of moves should be practised with ever-reducing application of the aids until the dog will respond to the command only.

Leaving your Dog

With all the commands now firmly established on the lead, on the spot, the next step is to begin to move away from your dog. Of course, his natural reaction will be to come with you. A simple solution might be to place some form of barrier in front of the dog or to carry out the exercise at the top of a flight of steps or on a stage. However, such measures will usually result in the dog moving as far forward as possible until he is physically unable to take up the next position, and this can be a cause of apprehension – the dog knows what is required but is unable to respond. If this is accompanied by correction from the handler in the form of extra commands or even chastisement, all the fun will go from the exercise, and all your good basic groundwork will be wasted. It is better to provide restraint from behind, which can be used at varying distances in a similar way to the lead. Fix a hook or a pulley to a tree in the garden, or the garden gate, about 3ft (1m) from the ground, fix a lead clip to a long length of string, and pass it over the hook.

To begin with, using the string in the same way as the lead, practise the positions close to your dog where you can apply all the other aids. Gradually begin to move away from your dog, relying only on the string to help with your commands, although you may still add the other body signals, such as raising your leg for the Down or sliding your left foot forward for the Stand. None the less, always maintain the slight tension on the lead to ensure a backward Sit from the Stand and from the Down. You will, of course, need to let the string go slack when giving the Down from the Stand or the Sit, but it can be used again to good effect when going back into the Sit or Stand.

Eventually you will be able to pretend to clip on the string but not do so, and after giving a little tug backward on the collar, leave your dog and carry out half a dozen positions without him being aware that he is now free to move forward. After many weeks, or even months, almost suddenly in the end, you will find that you have a happy, relaxed, reliable and movement-free Distance Control.

The aids just outlined may be adapted easily in teaching the Advanced Positions in Heelwork when you need them, but A.S.S.D. should be left as late as possible. If introduced too soon in Heelwork they can easily cause apprehension and lack of confidence, resulting in lagging or even stopping. Good, well-defined normal, slow, and fast paces must be well established before teaching positions on the move, which is why they have been left until the last training chapter in this book (*see* chap. 10).

Problems and Solutions

Stays

The question we are often asked is 'Will teaching Distant Control and Stays at the same time in the dog's life create confusion?' There is this possibility, but it is more likely that if you leave Distant Control until later and you already have your Stays reliably established, the new exercise will create confusion. This is what happened to our first Class C dog. Leaving Distant Control until we needed it for Class C had a catastrophic effect on his Stays. The ensuing confusion led to frequent movement in the Stays until the difference became properly established in his mind. Providing that you make it absolutely clear which of the two exercises you are doing at the commencement – using the command 'Control' or 'Stays' – confusion should be avoided. However, to make absolutely sure, you can train your Distant Control on Monday and Tuesday and practise Stays on Thursday and Friday.

Missed Positions

To avoid missing any of the six required positions, concentrate on clear diction, and your timing of the aids. Ensure that the aid is applied just after the command.

Forward Movement

If your dog displays a tendency to move forward, concentrate on the application of the aids which encourage slight backward movement. Also, spend much more time using the cord and pulley.

Basics to Remember

- When teaching the exercise, or setting your dog up in the ring, precede your last command to 'Wait' by telling your dog which exercise he is about to do. We say 'Control'.
- When you give your last command before leaving your dog say 'Wait' or say the position in which you wish your dog to remain while you walk away, i.e. say 'Stand' if you are leaving your dog in that position.
- In training, try to ensure that your dog's attention remains exclusively on you while you are walking away. Command 'Watch me' the instant he looks away.
- When you have turned to face your dog, the six positions will usually be communicated to you on a card that is handed to you by the steward. Hold it in such a way that you can read from position to position without excessive head or hand movement, or you may be penalized for an extra command.
- Remember to cultivate three different tones of voice for the three different commands, each making full use of the vowels sounds: a deep sonorous 'Down', a crisp even 'Sit', and a bright almost singing 'Stand'. The use of the dog's name in front of the Stand in the same bright tone is very important; you may also find it beneficial to use his name in front of the other two. If you do, remember to use the same tone in the name as you are about to use for the command itself. Also do not change or use variations of your dog's name for the separate commands, i.e. 'Tim Sit' and 'Timmy Stand'. Many judges, quite correctly in our opinion, will regard this as overstepping the intentions of the rules and mark for extra commands.
- If your dog misses a position in the ring or in training, it is bad practice to return to, and correct, your dog as this can soon create apprehension: this is quite a sensitive exercise, and your dog will soon become unsure whether you are returning to complete the exercise or just to correct him. This is how movement on Return sets in. It is better to give another, perhaps simpler, position at a distance, return to your dog, and praise him for being correct, and then go back to basics carrying out a few positions on the spot before leaving him to start again.
- Finally, when you have completed the six positions and returned to your dog, do not break the exercise too quickly. On the command from the steward 'Exercise finished', quietly tell your dog to wait, walk round him anti-clockwise back to the Heel position, bend over and praise quietly, and break the exercise backward before playing or praising more profusely.

CHAPTER 3

The Stays and Temperament Test

There is one group of exercises where play, excitement, and energy can not play too great a part. Nevertheless a high degree of concentration and the desire to please are still all-important.

The Exercise

On first impression this set of exercises might appear to be the easiest to learn or teach, for the dog is simply required to do nothing. Of course nothing is quite as straightforward as that, because the bond that you have been looking to achieve between you and your dog creates the desire in him to be with you at all times. When you command your dog to 'Stay' and 'Walk away', the urge to join you or persuade you to return is what creates problems.

In Beginners and Novice the dog must stay in the Sit for a period of one minute while the handler remains a few yards away though still in sight. In Class A the dog must stay in the Sit position for two minutes with the handler still in sight, but must stay for five minutes in the Down position while the handler walks away out of sight. In Class B a one-minute Stand-stay is introduced with the handler remaining in sight, though here the two-minute Sit-stay is carried out with the handler out of sight as well as for the five-minute Down. In Class C the Stand-stay is omitted, bearing in mind that there is the Distance Control at this level; the two-minute out-of-sight Sit still applies, but the Down-stay out of sight is extended to ten minutes.

Marks are deducted for the dog breaking the allocated position, but they are graduated so that the earlier in the allocated time the dog moves, the more the marks that are deducted.

A clear break from the correct position to another, i.e. from the Sit to the Down, or from the allocated position to follow the handler is easy to identify and will carry a proportional penalty, but minor errors can also be marginally penalized. These include creeping along the ground whilst in the Down or moving a paw or two in the Stand. It is important, therefore, to insist right from the start on as near perfect stillness as is possible.

Teaching the Exercise

We have already mentioned that the command 'Stay' should be reserved for this exercise only. The commands 'Wait' or 'Sit' should mean 'Wait in that position until you are told to do something else: come, fetch, find, etc.' The command 'Stay' can now mean 'Stay until I return and the exercise is completed'.

Even in Beginners and Novice there is a last command, after which further commands or signals from the handler to ensure that the dog maintains his position will be heavily penalized. However, when you begin to train the Stays, do not immediately give a last command.

The Sit

We begin by teaching the Sit. Set the dog up in the Sit position as described at the commencement of teaching Novice Recall (*see* p. 18), on the lead with the end in the right hand passing over the left hand, which is there to offer backward and upward restraint.

Command your dog to 'Sit' and 'Stay', and leave (with the right foot as usual). Take one pace, and turn to semi-face your dog. The left hand is under the lead as in early Novice Recall to ensure that at the slightest sign of movement it is able to move upward and backward, this time with the command 'Stay' to ensure the dog maintains his position.

Even if the dog does not show any signs of moving, in the early stages keep repeating the Stay command accompanied by praise. This can be gradually reduced to zero over the period of just a few days. At the same time, the left hand can be lowered so that it becomes less and less obvious as a restraint. If your dog will maintain the position for just ten to fifteen seconds to begin with, return to his side then quietly walk anti-clockwise round your dog, still using the lead as necessary to maintain the position. Bend over and quietly praise while he is still in the Sit, and break the exercise.

One of the secrets of a confident reliable Stay is not to be in too much of a hurry to do a full-scale sequence. Even in the next stage, when you take the lead off, you should revert to repeating the 'Stay' command as you increase the distance that you leave between you and your dog. When you are able to leave a space of between eight and ten paces, you may again gradually reduce your Stay commands. You should return to your dog within fifteen seconds or so to begin with, but over a period of a few days you may begin to build up the time away from him to one minute. Do not go beyond this time for the moment.

Another golden rule to remember is 'Better a fifteen-second Stay completed correctly than a two-minute Stay with the dog breaking before you return'. Ten or fifteen half-minute Stays practised and completed correctly during a day are much more beneficial than one five-minute Stay attempted and broken at four-and-a-half minutes.

The Down-Stay

When a reliable one-minute stay in sight but without commands has been perfected, you may turn your attention to the Down. Begin back on the lead. Down your dog by putting your foot on the lead as described in Distance Control (*see* chap. 2). Say 'Stay', and step away only with the right foot so that the left foot remains on the lead restraining the dog. You only need to be this one pace away from your dog to begin with, and keep repeating your 'Stay' command with quiet praise, reducing only gradually to nothing. At the same time as the dog's confidence appears to grow, you may remove your foot from the lead, but be ready to replace it if the dog shows any sign of moving. Build up the time spent away from the dog gradually, returning after only ten to fifteen seconds to begin with. Apply the same procedure for breaking the exercise as for the Sit, i.e. walk round the dog before quietly praising, this time in the Down.

When you attempt the exercise lead free, remember to revert to repeated 'Stay' commands with quiet praise as you increase time and distance, reducing them gradually as the dog's confidence becomes more and more evident.

There is a school of thought which believes that the dog should be compelled to carry out the Down-stay in the flat position, that is to say the dog lies flat on his side with his legs outstretched at the side and his head flat on the ground as if asleep. The theory is that he becomes more settled than when lying in the simple Down position. In our opinion, there is a danger here that in the long Class B or Class C Down the dog may drift off to sleep; if there is any sudden noise, such as a prize award in an adjacent ring, the dog may be startled from sleep and jump up. We only teach our dogs the Down in the normal, comfortable position they first adopt when given the command.

Stand-Stay

Stand-stay.

Aid reduced to almost nothing at this stage.

The Stand-Stay

The 'Stand-Stay' is not required until you graduate into Class B, so you can afford to take your time to teach and establish reliability in this one. To begin with, on the lead, give your dog the Stand command and apply the aids as described for Distance Control (*see* chap. 2). Tell your dog to 'Stay' while keeping your left foot under his tummy (not making contact) to maintain the position. Repeat your Stay command with quiet praise frequently.

It is more difficult to maintain an aid while beginning to move away from your dog, and your dog will still be unsure exactly what is required. The tendency to revert to the Sit is difficult to overcome. In the early stages you will have to find a substitute aid to replace the left foot position. A plank of wood about 8–9in (20–23cm) wide which can be propped up on a couple of sticks is ideal. Having set your dog up as usual in the Stand, fit the plank under

your dog's tummy so that his front legs are in front of it and his hind legs are behind. This takes the place of your left foot, and you can take a pace away while still using the lead, repeating your Stand command with praise.

There are two ways to progress from this point. Firstly, you can leave your plank in position while you increase time and distance, maintaining commands for the time being. Secondly, you can reduce the depth of your plank until it is no more than a fine stick, while staying close to your dog.

Now your dog has confidence to maintain the Stand at a distance with a well-defined aid, or confidence to maintain the Stand while you are close with little or no aid. The next logical step, of course, is to begin to combine the two, using ever-decreasing depths of plank with ever-increasing distance. At the same time you can begin to reduce the frequency of commands and praise. Do not forget to take your time with this exercise.

When you have finally achieved a confident Sit, Down and Stand-stay, you now have to introduce to the Sit and the Down the out-of-sight element. Following our theme of simplicity, clearly all that you have to do is to leave your dog, initially in familiar surroundings and walk out of sight for a few seconds to begin with. The secret is not to push your luck by increasing your time out of sight too much too soon.

Much of this early training can be carried out when you and your dog are alone, but it is a group exercise, so you will soon need to begin practising at a club with other dogs. As long as the dogs around your youngster are experienced and reliable in the Stays and of sound temperament, his own confidence will be enhanced by doing Stays in company.

The Temperament Test

Falling under the broad sphere of influence of Stays in training terms, although it is not regarded as a Stay exercise, is the Temperament Test. Applicable only to Novice (on the lead) and Class A (off the lead), the exercise is designed to ensure that the worst extremes of temperament – severe aggression or nervousness – can be highlighted and brought under control. In our opinion there are very few dogs who should be penalized under the Temperament Test because a dog who exhibits any reservations about being approached and handled by a complete stranger should not necessarily be branded as having a suspect temperament. Only dogs who exhibit serious aggression should be penalized, in our view. At this extreme, all marks should be deducted.

The exercise progresses as follows. The dog is set up in the Stand position; the judge then approaches the dog and makes light contact by passing his hand over the dog's head and back. This is not a Stand-stay, and the dog should not be penalized if he subsides into the Sit. Some judges may deduct marks if the dog becomes too exuberant and jumps up, although

we would not. In Novice, the handler may continue to talk to the dog, but in Class A the exercise commences with a 'Last command'.

In training, the exercise is introduced during Stays that are conducted in a group. At the end of the Sit to begin with and then the Stand-stay, handlers return not immediately to their own dogs but to the one next to them. After quietly stroking this dog, they return to their own. In this way the dog becomes used to being approached by someone who is fairly unfamiliar. The Temperament Test should present no problem at all if your dog has been thoroughly socialized as a young puppy. However, if you have acquired a dog that has spent much of his formative weeks or months in an isolated situation, or you have a 'rescue' dog whose earlier life has been subject to cruelty or neglect, then you will have to spend much more time on this exercise – softly, softly, through semi-familiar people before bringing in complete strangers is the only way.

Problems and Solutions

Movement

'I can't stop my dog moving in the Stays' is a plaintive cry we hear from time to time. Dogs move in the Stays for one of four reasons. Your dog may lack confidence and will therefore want to be with you at all times. He will follow you or move, risking correction or even chastisement, in order to persuade you to return. We call this Handlers' Recall. To solve this problem, go back to basics with short Stays completed correctly. You might even revert to extra commands and praise. It is better to complete ten fifteen-second Stays correctly spread throughout the day than one five-minute Stay incorrectly.

Another reason why dogs move in Stays is simple lack of concentration or laziness. If this is the case, go back to first principles and short Stays, but you may have to think about being firmer in your attitude – not just in your Stays, but in your general relationship with your dog. If your dog appears to lack the concentration required to maintain the Sit and flops into the Down before the one or two minutes have expired, when setting up before 'Last command', tell your dog to 'Sit', and say no more, gently pressing down on his neck. Your dog will then tend to drop into the Down, at which time you can lift him back into the Sit through his collar and say 'No', 'Sit'. After doing this once or twice, you will find the dog quite strongly resists the pressure to go down at which time you can praise. This concentration should carry your dog through the one or two minutes' Sit period.

Yet another reason for movement is a dog's inability to resist some sort of distraction outside the ring. Applause from a prize presentation in an adjacent ring is a common cause, or someone playing with his dog in the immediate vicinity. When training for Stays at a club or in a group, it is important to introduce such distractions to get your dog used to them, but do it very gradually. One person clapping quietly to begin with can be built up to a group clapping and cheering more loudly over a period of several weeks.

Lastly, movement can result from a more unpredictable form of distraction which is more difficult to simulate and train for – a sudden clap of thunder or burst of gunfire for instance. Very hot weather can also have an effect on your dog's concentration. If this happens, you are best just to 'take it on the chin'. It doesn't happen very often, and attempting to train for it could create more problems than it solves. A sudden burst of rainfall could be trained against by making your dog do Stays under a hose pipe shower, but is it worth it?

CHAPTER 4

Finishes

When your dog has returned to the Present position in Novice Recall, Retrieve, and Scent, at all levels the exercise is completed on instruction from the steward – 'Finish' – by the dog being commanded back to the Sit at heel position on the left-hand side. There are two accepted manoeuvres for the Finish. The dog may pass clockwise behind the handler or tuck in directly anti-clockwise to the left. From either direction the dog should end in the Sit at heel position. Marks will be deducted if the dog reacts slowly, passes excessively wide on either side of the handler, or sits crooked, forward or backward of the correct position.

We teach and train the Finish separately from its associated exercises and refrain from completing the Finish in training until after the dog has presented in Novice Recall, Retrieve, and Scent in order to prevent the habit of anticipation forming. In addition to the tendency to anticipate the Finish, the dog may also develop the habit of presenting persistently crooked, pointing in the direction in which he expects to finish.

Right-hand Finish. Command 'Heel'. Lead behind right knee and held in left hand.

Teaching the Right-Hand Finish

Our simplified breakdown in teaching this exercise is as follows.

Step One

With your dog sitting at heel on the lead, command him to 'Wait', and walk round to the Present position. Take one pace to your left and one pace forward so that your dog is now sitting on your right-hand side facing behind you. Gently pass your lead behind you, encouraging your dog to wait if necessary. Hold your lead in your left hand.

The dog now has only to complete half the distance round you into the finished Sit at heel position. This is achieved by giving your right-hand Finish command. Say 'Close' as your dog is expected to pass around you similarly to a Right About-turn. You may elect to accompany

41

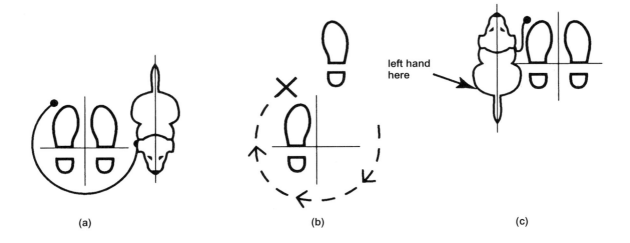

(a)   (b)   (c)

Right-hand Finish – stage 1: (a) From Present position, take one pace to the left and one pace forward; pass lead behind and hold in right hand. (b) Command 'Close'; pace forward with right foot; gather up lead as dog follows dotted line. (c) Bring left foot forward to right, command 'Sit' while using left hand to press dog into Sit position.

your dog's name with a signal. Obviously a downward backward movement with your right hand will encourage your dog to finish clockwise or right-handed. At the same time take one pace forward on your right foot accompanied by a light pull on the lead. As the dog follows you round, transfer the lead into your right hand, follow left foot up to right, say 'Sit', and reach down and place the dog into the correct Sit position.

Step Two

With your dog sitting at heel still on the lead, command him to 'Wait' and walk round to the Present position. This time gently pass your lead behind you, so that it hangs just behind and level with your right knee. Hold the lead in your left hand. When you give your right-hand Finish command this time, take a pace back with your right foot so that the tension on the lead encourages the dog to commence his passage round you. Place your right foot back up to the left, transfer the lead to your right hand, say 'Sit', and reach down with your left

hand to place your dog into the correct Sit position.

Step Three

When the dog will respond automatically to the right-hand Finish command or signal, commencing again from the Present position, let your lead loop down in front of you, give your command or signal, and as your dog responds let him carry the lead around so that he maintains a close circuit around, avoiding the tendency to go wide.

Teaching the Left-Hand Finish

Step One

With your dog on the lead at the Sit at heel position, tell your dog to 'Sit' or 'Wait', and turn so that he is sitting square to and pointing toward your left leg with the end of the lead in your right hand passing over your left which is

42

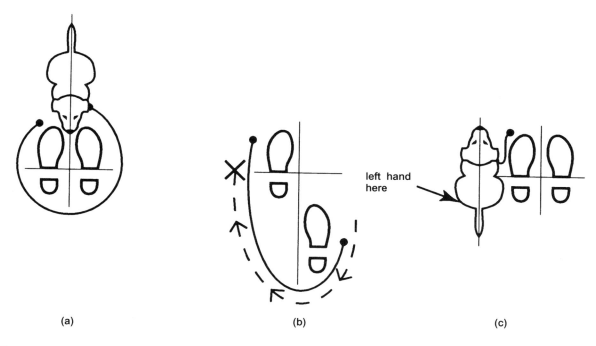

(a) (b) (c)

left hand here

Right-hand Finish – stage 2: (a) Dog in Present position with lead passed behind handler's knee.
(b) Command 'Close'; step back with right foot, creating tension on the lead to draw dog with it. (c) Bring right foot forward to left; command 'Sit' while using left hand to press dog into Sit position.

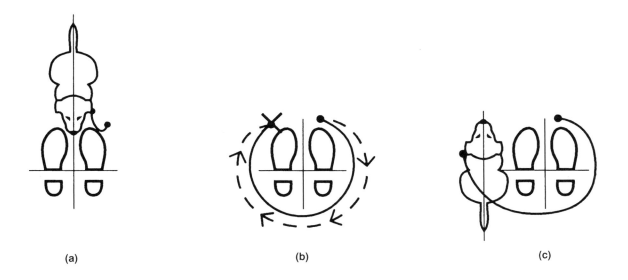

(a) (b) (c)

Right-hand Finish – stage 3: (a) Dog in Present position with lead handing loose in front of handler.
(b) Command 'Close'; dog draws lead with him as he travels round handler, thus ensuring close finish.
(c) Command 'Sit', while using left hand to press dog into position.

43

*Left-hand Finish. Command 'Heel'. Move your
left leg back; slide your left hand down the lead in
a backwards direction in line with your leg. Don't
bring your leg or hand forwards again until the
dog has fully responded.*

used to maintain the Sit until you give your
next command. Here again the dog has only to
complete half the manoeuvre to begin with.

Your left-hand Finish command can be
'Heel' or 'In' or you can use a signal downward and backward with your left hand.
Having given your command or signal, take a
pace back with your left foot, and draw your
dog back until he has turned, then bring your
foot back, reach down and place your dog into
the Sit at heel.

Step Two

From the Sit at heel, on the command 'Wait',
turn to the Present position and take a pace to
the right and one pace forward. Following your
left-hand Finish command or signal, take a
pace back with your left foot, draw your dog
back with the lead, reach down, and place him
into the Sit at heel position.

Step Three

You can now attempt the Finish from the Pre-

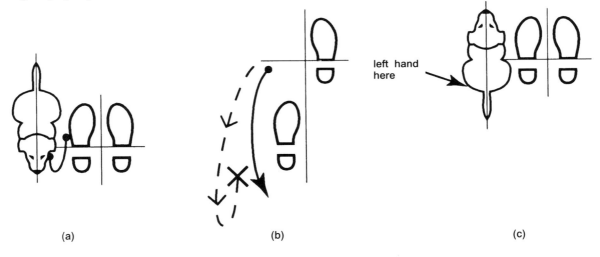

left hand
here

(a)　　　　　　　　(b)　　　　　　　　(c)

Left-hand Finish – stage 1: (a) From the Present position, take one pace to the right and one pace
forward. (b) Command 'In'; step back with left foot and draw dog back with your left hand; wait until dog
has responded. (c) When dog has moved back up to heel, bring left foot back up to right; command 'Sit',
while using left hand to press dog into Sit position.

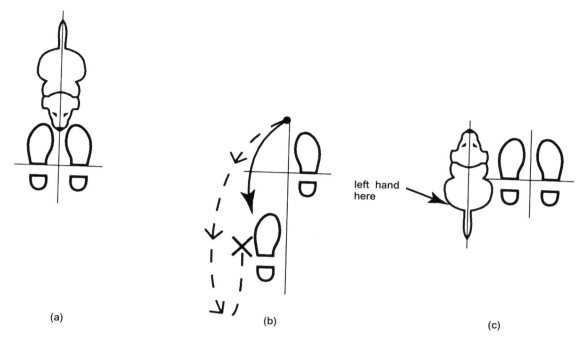

(a)   (b)   (c)

Left-hand Finish – stage 2: (a) Commence in Present position. (b) Command 'In'; step back with left foot and draw dog back with your left hand; wait until dog has responded. (c) Bring left foot back up to right; command 'Sit' while using left hand to press dog into Sit position.

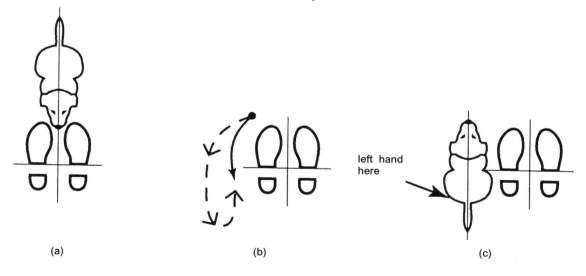

(a)   (b)   (c)

Left-hand Finish – stage 3: (a) Commence with dog in Present position. (b) Command 'In', as in stage 2, but keep your feet still; instead make nominal hand movement backward. (c) When dog has responded, command 'Sit' while using left hand to place dog in Sit position.

sent position. After giving your command or signal, still take your step back and use your hand in the lead to bring your dog back. From this stage, the step back can gradually be reduced until it is no longer required and your hand in the lead can also be reduced until (if you have selected a signal) all you have to do is move your hand quickly downward and backwards. If you find a command suits your dog better, the hand signal will have to be reduced further until it is non-existent.

You now have two alternative Finishes. No doubt, after a while, one will evolve as the most consistent and accurate for your dog, but you should continue to train and practise both as this will help to prevent the tendency for your dog to Present with a bias in the direction which through habit he expects to finish.

CHAPTER 5

Heelwork Proper

Now you have an instinctive and accurate Novice Recall and undivided attention in simple Heelwork in a circle. While these two great attributes are being cultivated, your own attention can begin to turn to Heelwork proper which will, of course, include turns.

The Exercise

From Beginners to Class C, Heelwork forms the major part of all the tests, and it is the exercise which gives you the greatest opportunity to make your mark. Starting from the Halt with the dog at the Sit on the handler's left-hand side, on command from the steward, dog and handler set off together. The dog is required to maintain his position at the handler's side with his shoulder level with, and comfortably close to, the handler's leg. Deviation from this position in any direction will result in penalty marks being deducted, i.e. lagging behind, forward working, wide, too close, or impeding.

The Heelwork route or pattern is predetermined by the judge of the day and is the same for each dog and handler in that class. The changes of direction or turns are communicated to the handler by the judge's steward who calls out the appropriate commands – 'Right Turn', 'Left Turn', 'About-Turn', 'Halt' etc. – at the designated points in the ring. Typical Heelwork patterns for a Novice Test and a more advanced Class C are indicated in the diagrams.

The dog is required to maintain the correct position in relation to his handler throughout the turns. If the dog has not been taught prop-

erly and is not giving full attention, it is easy for him to drift wide on Right Turns or About-turns or bump into his handler's leg on Left Turns. On command from the steward, dog and handler should come to a Halt together with the dog in the Sit.

The dog is required to be 'straight', that is to say with his spine straight and parallel to the direction of travel. Any apparent inward or outward misalignment is interpreted as a 'crooked Sit' and marked down accordingly. The dog's shoulder position forward, backward, or wide of the handler's leg will also be penalized.

From Beginners to Class A, the Heelwork is carried out both on and off the lead. The lead must always be slack, however. Use of the lead to maintain the dog's position – 'tight lead' – will be quite heavily penalized. Class B and C Heelwork is all lead free.

Upon commencement of the exercise and the steward's command 'Forward', the dog's name accompanied by a command may be used to set off. In Beginners and Novice only, further commands and encouragement may be used to ensure that the dog keeps up and maintains the correct position, but from Class A upward any further commands or signals must be penalized. Similarly upon the steward's command to 'Halt', in Beginners and Novice, commands and/or signals may be used to ensure compliance and accuracy from the dog; in A and above the dog should sit correctly unaided by command or signal.

In Classes B and C, the Heelwork is conducted not just at normal walking pace but also at slow and fast paces, and there must be a very clear distinction between the three. In

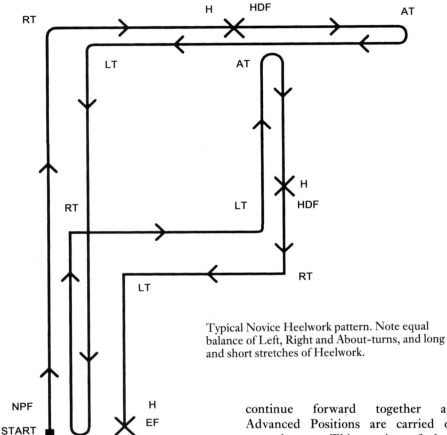

Typical Novice Heelwork pattern. Note equal balance of Left, Right and About-turns, and long and short stretches of Heelwork.

Class B each change of pace must commence from a Halt, but in Class C a change from one pace to another may be required to be made on the move. If so, no command may be given without incurring a penalty.

Finally, in Class C only, there is also what is known as the Advanced Positions on the move. In this advanced extension of the exercise, the dog is required to take up the Sit, Down, and Stand positions in the order prescribed by the judge while the handler continues forward alone until the route indicated by the steward brings him back to the position where the dog was left, at which point (the 'pick-up') they

continue forward together again. The Advanced Positions are carried out only at normal pace. This section of the exercise is very specialized and requires special attention – but at a later time in your training programme, the reasons for which are explained in chapter 10.

Penalty points in Heelwork are likely to be as a result of the following. The dog might deviate from the correct position on the move by drifting wide, either when proceeding in a straight line or on turns. He might work too close (impeding the handler), make contact on left turns ('kneeing'), hang back (this tends to occur mainly in fast pace) or work forward (the dog tends to 'take over'). Alternatively, the dog might not adopt the correct position at the Halt. He might make a crooked Sit, forward Sit, backward Sit, wide Sit, slow Sit, Overshoot, or a combination of two or more of

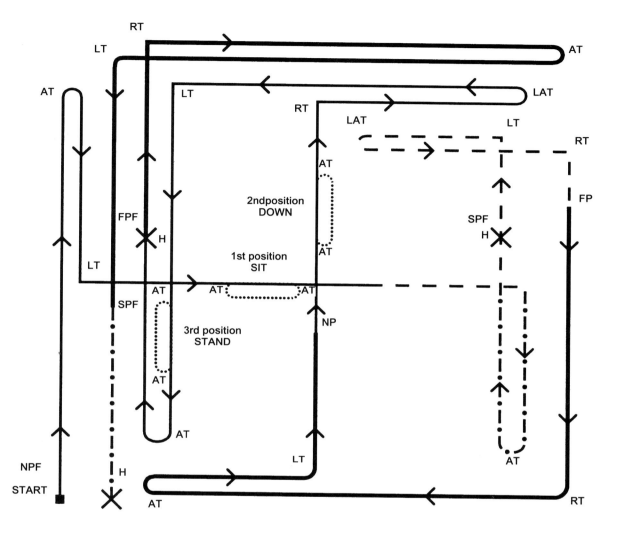

Typical Class C Heelwork pattern. This is much more complicated, but there is still an equal balance of turns and long and short stretches of Heelwork.

these. Beyond Beginners or Novice, extra commands from the handler – given consciously or subconsciously by word or signal – will lose points.

Anticipation in the form of responding prematurely to any of the commands – particularly steward's commands – or moving too soon on pick-up from the Heelwork positions is another reason to deduct points, as is not responding to

any of the commands or delay in pick-up. Lastly, the handler might be responsible for lost points by not responding correctly or in sufficient time to the steward's commands.

The severity of penalization depends on the extent of deviation from perfection. Obviously major faults like missed positions, consistent lagging or consistent forward work will incur very significant penalty marks.

Teaching the Exercise

You now need to progress in Heelwork from the left-hand circle to the introduction of straight lines and turns. The key to a smooth transition is correct and consistent footwork, combined with good timing of commands to indicate to the dog in which direction you intend to turn. This applies particularly in the dog's formative days and weeks in Novice, when a command is also allowed in the ring, but in fact when training even an experienced dog one should regularly revert to Novice work, with commands.

There are three steps to perfecting each turn (Right, About, Left and even Left-About). They are as follows. First, form the habit of correct footwork without your dog so that it becomes second nature without even thinking about it. Second, teach the dog on the spot using the correct footwork together with other helpful aids and commands. Third, introduce turns on the move. It is at this stage that the timing of your commands is of paramount importance.

The Use and Timing of Commands in Heelwork

To maximize the effectiveness of your command select one word for Right and Right About-turns and another word for Left (or Left About-turns). It does not matter what you choose as long as you are consistent, but we will say 'Close' for Right and Right About and 'In' for Left or Left About.

A common downfall, even among many experienced handlers, is excessive and wasteful use of the dog's name preceding the command. With the exception of training on the spot, when it may be necessary to precede a command with the dog's name to instigate initial movement from a stationary position, the use of your dog's name in front of the Turn command is in the most literal sense a 'waste of time' for two reasons.

Firstly, if you have chosen different commands to precede a Right or Left Turn, the use of the same name in front of each dilutes its effectiveness. 'Jacko Close' and 'Jacko In' lack the distinction of 'Close' and 'In'. Secondly, by the time you have said your dog's name, you have wasted a split second in communicating the actual command to the dog's brain, and he therefore has that much less time to react. By the time you have said both name and command, you may find yourself already turning with the consequence that the dog is surprised and makes a mistake, which requires correction. This is, in our opinion, where the rot most often sets in. Let the first thing that your dog hears, a moment before you do it, be the correct command. Timing is everything.

The Right Turn

Let us begin with the easy turn first, the Right Turn, and begin with footwork without the dog. The left foot is the one nearest the dog,

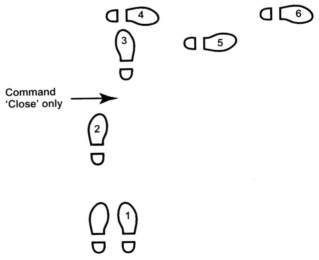

The Right Turn. Pattern applied at all paces – slow, normal and fast. With this and other similar manoeuvres, do not precede commands with the dog's name.

50

and so we believe that for each turn it is the left foot that should point the way.

Stand with your feet together and set off at a slow pace (as if with your dog) with your left foot. As your right foot touches the ground, place your left foot across the front of your right foot to form a letter 'T' and step straight out with your right foot at 90 degrees to the direction you started in. Thus, the sequence becomes left foot, right foot, 'T', straight out. The moment when the right foot is about to be placed is the latest chance for your command 'Close' – any later and you will almost certainly catch your dog out. Remember, practise: left, 'Close', right, ('T'), straight out; left, right, 'Close', ('T'), straight out, again and again until the footwork is subconscious, and the command is automatic.

The About-Turn

The About-turn now becomes an extension of the Right Turn. The direction of the turn is the same so the command and its timing remain, and – up to the first 'T' – the footwork is the same.

Starting again with footwork – without the dog – set off from the Halt: left, 'Close', right, 'T', then place the right foot to produce another 'T' shape pointing back the way you came. Then step straight out with your left foot. As you are bringing your left foot round and through to step off, it is advisable to repeat your 'Close' command.

It always amazes us how many Beginner/Novice handlers, having used one command, completely give up for the rest of the turn,

The About-turn. Pattern applied at all paces – slow, normal and fast.

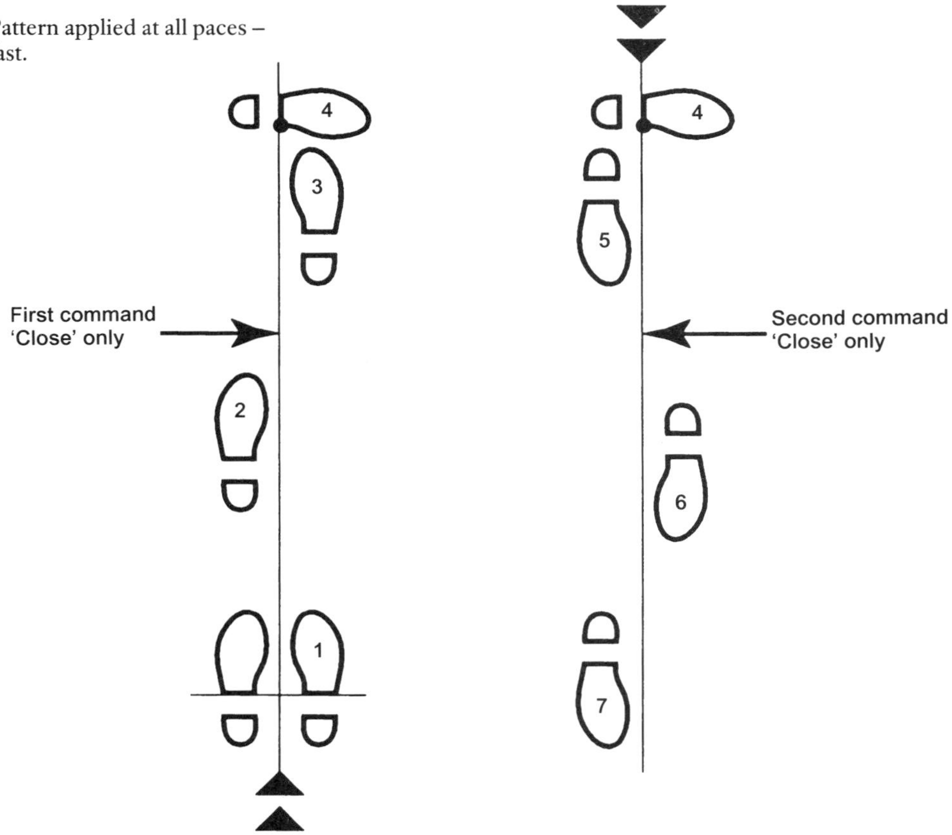

First command 'Close' only

Second command 'Close' only

leaving the dog to his own devices; for the young inexperienced dog especially, a second command as you are just completing the turn is vital to maintain concentration. First attempts with the dog should be at the Halt, so it will be necessary to precede the command with the dog's name at the Halt only. With your dog at the Sit beside you, say his name in a bright tone followed by the 'Close' command. Immediately following the command, place your left foot across your right to form the first 'T', place your right foot to form the second 'T', place your left foot beside your right, reach down with the left hand to place your dog into the Sit, and praise.

When the response on the spot is satisfactory and consistent, the manoeuvre can be attempted on the move, first at slow pace and then at normal. Remember that only the command should be used, somewhere between left foot and right, before forming the first 'T'. As the

second 'T' is formed, repeat the command with slightly increased emphasis. The final foot placings and commands would be left, 'Close', right, 'T', 'T', 'Close', straight out with left, repeated again until all commands and footwork come absolutely automatically.

When you are working your dog at a club, indoors, if you have the side of the room immediately on your right when you do an About-turn, the dog is less likely to go wide as the turn is completed because there is little room to do so and there are no distractions. If you do an About-turn with the wall on your left, there will be a large open space into which the dog is turning and the distraction of other dogs and people. Remember then that you will have to work much harder with your second command to ensure that the dog stays close and does not go wide.

The Left Turn

Almost everyone finds the Left Turn more difficult to master than the Right.

Practise footwork first, without your dog. Again, it is the left foot that points the way. Begin as usual with your feet together, and set off with the left foot. As, or just before, the right foot comes to the ground you should give the command (we say 'In'), and here it is most important to remember not to precede the command with the dog's name. On Right or Right About-turns it may not do too much harm for it is an attention getter and can have much the same effect as the 'Close' command itself, but on a left turn the use of the dog's name does much more to negate the effectiveness of the command itself and has the effect of bringing the dog's head over to the right foot just as you begin to turn left, which usually results in contact ('kneeing') so let the first thing the dog hears be the command, well in advance of the commencement of the turn.

Having given the command as the right foot comes to the ground, place your left foot (pointing left) across your right foot to form a

Close About-turn.

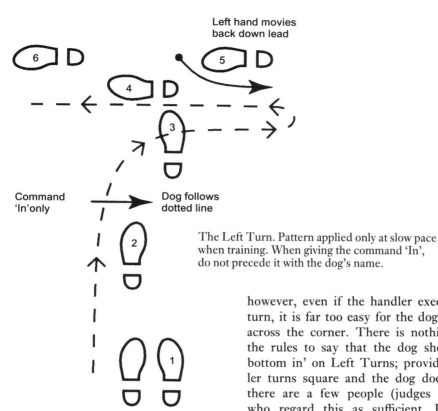

Left hand movies
back down lead

Command
'In'only

Dog follows
dotted line

The Left Turn. Pattern applied only at slow pace
when training. When giving the command 'In',
do not precede it with the dog's name.

'T', and then step straight out to the left with your right foot. This may feel awkward at first, but it is important that the left foot is placed to form a 'T' rather than an inverted 'L' so as to avoid obstructing the dog; you will find the whole manoeuvre easier to carry out if you allow both knees to flex slightly as you do it. In sequence then, from the Halt, we have left, 'In', right, 'T', straight out, first at slow then at normal pace. Even without the dog, you should practise the timing of the command.

Next, you should practise with your dog on the spot. Here we introduce an additional manoeuvre to ensure that the dog learns early to 'tuck in' or 'square off' on the left turn.

If we return for the moment to the Right Turn, it can be seen that if the handler turns square at 90 degrees it is almost impossible for the dog not to do likewise; on the Left Turn,

however, even if the handler executes a square turn, it is far too easy for the dog simply to cut across the corner. There is nothing specific in the rules to say that the dog should 'tuck his bottom in' on Left Turns; providing the handler turns square and the dog does not impede there are a few people (judges and handlers) who regard this as sufficient. However, this somewhat sloppy interpretation of the rules always creates a very fine distinction between what does and does not constitute a 'left wheel' (a markable offence). Over the last few years, therefore, most discerning handlers have taken more care to ensure that their precise Left Turns are reflected in their dog's action. To do this effectively the dog is encouraged in training to tuck his rear end backward and in on the spot and at slow pace.

We must stress that this action should not be taught to the young dog at normal pace. It should be perfected on the spot and at slow pace; if the actions and aids we are about to cover are carried through into normal pace too soon, the dog's impulsion will be lost and he will lag behind out of the turn. If this is accompanied by a jerk up on the lead to bring the dog back to the correct position, this amounts to 'training by default', resulting in apprehension and loss of enthusiasm.

Tuck-in on Left Turn.

If the dog is correctly schooled on the spot, at a slow pace, and if you time your command correctly (early enough) you will soon find that your dog gradually begins to tuck in at normal pace without any loss of impulsion.

Having accepted the need for caution with normal pace, you are now ready to begin training on the spot. With your dog on the lead, in the Sit, at your left-hand side, using his name only to encourage him onto his feet, give your Left Turn command ('In'), place your left foot across your right to form a 'T' (left foot pointing left), then step back with your right foot and at the same time draw your left hand backward down the lead to encourage your dog backward as he turns. Maintain this position until your dog has responded and moves his rear end backwards as he has turned, then bring your right foot back to the side of your left, say 'Sit', and reach down and praise your dog. Thus, the complete manoeuvre is, from the halt, dog's name, command 'In', place the left foot to form 'T', back with right foot and left hand in lead. When the dog responds, right foot back up to left, reach down, and place dog into Sit.

The progression to forward movement at slow pace now is very simple. Commence from the Halt. Set off with the dog's name and 'Heel' command. The progression is left foot, command 'In', right foot, form 'T' with left foot across right, and pace back with right foot, at the same time tucking the dog in with the left hand down the lead. When satisfied that the dog has responded sufficiently, carry the right foot forward as stepping out of the turn. Repeat until footwork, handwork, and timing of command are second nature. Then you can progress to normal pace, but remember that the step back with the right foot must be abandoned and the draw back with the left hand must be reduced to a mere touch.

At normal pace we now have, as we approach the turn, left foot, command 'In', right foot, 'T' (slight only backward inflection of the left hand down the lead), straight out with the right foot, and so on.

In this way you will soon have a dog that tucks in and turns square on left turns without loss of impulsion or enthusiasm. You will also by now have ingrained in your dog undivided attention, which means that he will be looking up and slightly across to the right. When you execute a Right Turn or Right About-turn, therefore, the dog is turning into or toward his general line of vision and is confident to do so while maintaining 100 per cent concentration on you. When turning left, however, the dog is turning away from his general line of vision, and the temptation for a young dog to look away to 'get his bearings' is very strong. A quick 'Watch me' command immediately following the Left Turn is, therefore, very important when training the young dog. Eventually, when you have both learned to sense one another's every breath and heartbeat, this command, like all the others, will cease to be necessary.

Here is a hint to sharpen up your Left

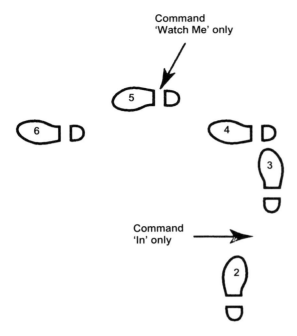

Command
'Watch Me' only

Command
'In' only

The Left Turn. Pattern applied at all paces –
slow, normal and fast – when the 'tuck in' has
been established.

C, you and your dog will encounter more intricate turns: the Left About, the Right About Right Turn, and even Left About Left Turn.

The Left About-Turn

The Left About-turn should not be introduced until you and your dog have perfected the Left Turn. It can be achieved in two ways.

The first is a direct extension of the Left Turn. Begin at slow pace. From the 'In' command as your right foot comes to the ground, place your left foot pointing left to form your 'T'. Apply the light 'tuck-in' restraint down the lead with your left hand. From there take your right foot completely round and over your left anti-clockwise and place it as your first step out in the opposite direction. Having perfected this manoeuvre at slow pace, exactly the same procedure is extended into normal. Although this is perhaps the smoothest of the two alternatives, it can soon be appreciated that it requires a fairly high degree of nimbleness or physical dexterity which not all of us may possess; the second alternative can be easier to execute and will appear just as smart if practised as a smooth continuous sequence.

Begin at slow pace. Give the 'In' command as the right foot comes down. Form the 'T' with your left foot, and place your right foot at the side of and parallel to it. Place your left foot to point back in the direction from which you have just come and step off with your right. There is a danger with this version of the Left About that you may be perceived as waiting for your dog and penalized accordingly, so you will have to practise to make it look both smooth and regulated.

Turns. Many people have difficulty in judging a square turn, so in spite of how well they may have schooled their dogs on the spot and at slow pace, they tend themselves to walk slightly away from their dogs as they turn. This means a left wheel is more evident than a square Left Turn. In order to discipline yourself into turning sharply, set out three markers as an equilateral triangle. This can be in the form of chalk marks on the training hall floor, or small pegs on the grass about ten paces apart. Beginning at slow pace but eventually building up to normal, with your dog, turn left at each marker leading toward the next. You will find after a little while that if you can turn left through 60 degrees you will have disciplined yourself to turn at 90 degrees much more precisely and confidently.

As you progress upward into Classes B and

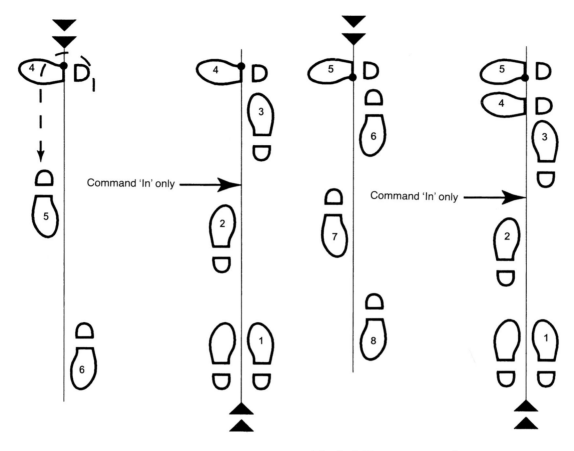

The Left About-turn – type 1.

The Left About-turn – type 2.

The Right About Right Turn

As with the Left About, the Right About Right Turn and Left About Left Turns should not be introduced until your more basic ones have been perfected. They are both, however, an extension of the About-turns from which they originate.

Going into the Right About Right Turn you will carry out the initial footwork as for an About-turn, all at slow pace of course to begin with, so the sequence will be command 'Close' as the right foot comes to the ground, form the first 'T' with your left foot, reverse the right foot to form the second 'T', then instead of

stepping out, form a third 'T', this time again with your left foot, and then step out with your right foot.

The About-turn Right Turn, once established in your Heelwork repertoire, is very useful for tightening up any tendency for the dog to drift wide coming out of turns. If you progress left-handed round a square (your training hall or a ring) by doing an About-turn Right Turn in each corner, you will be surprised after three or four of these how close your dog will stay on your next About-turn.

56

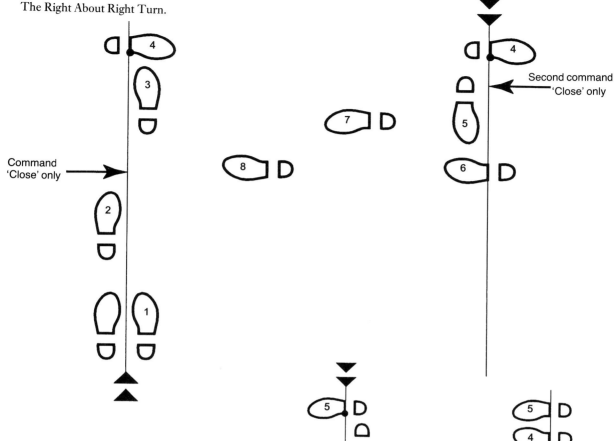

The Right About Right Turn.

Command 'Close' only

Second command 'Close' only

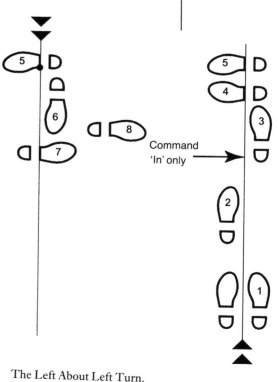

The Left About Left Turn.

The Left About Left Turn

Going into the Left About Left Turn you will carry out the initial footwork for a type 2 Left About, so the sequence will be command 'In' as the right foot comes down, form your first 'T' with your left foot, place your right foot parallel to the left, form your second 'T' with your left foot again, place your right foot parallel, form a third 'T' with your left foot, and step out. Achieving a smooth-flowing manoeuvre for this one at normal pace will take a great deal of practice, but in today's highly competitive and demanding scene at top level it won't be long before you encounter it.

The Left About Left Turn is also useful as an extra incentive to teach your dog to tuck in on left turns, but don't overdo things.

Command 'In' only

Halts

At predetermined points in the Heelwork pattern, you will be instructed by the steward to Halt, at which point you must come to a standstill with your dog in the Sit at heel position. The dog must be sitting in the correct, straight position.

In Beginners and Novice you may give commands and signals to achieve this, providing that you do not make contact with your dog. From Class A upward, the dog must assume the correct Sit position totally uncommanded. Penalty points will be deducted for crooked, backward, forward, wide, or slow Sits. In Class A and above any extra commands – voluntary or involuntary – given by the handler to achieve a correct Sit will also be penalized.

The secret of consistent straight correctly positioned Sits is repeated application of the three aids, or any single or double combination thereof, leaving the dog only very rarely to his own devices.

As in Presents in Novice Recall, etc., we want to encourage the dog to commence to Sit while he still has some forward impulsion, so we give the command aid 'Sit' just as the right foot comes to the ground. Then place your right foot and come to your Halt by bringing your left foot up to the right, and as you do this apply the other two-thirds of the Sit at heel aid: the right hand holding the lead is taken upward whilst the left hand presses (not slaps) the hind quarters of the dog downward and inward so that he completes the Sit firmly and snugly against the handler's left leg.

Even as the dog is in the Sit position, a repeated gentle press down the outside flank accompanied by praise reinforces the feeling in the dog of being in the right place. Any combination of one or more of these aids can be applied to Halts in training, but the most important is giving the 'Sit' command early enough to ensure that the dog begins to Sit while still moving forward.

Timing

When training under instruction, or working in the ring in Beginners and Novice, careful consideration should be given to the timing of your commands, not just in relation to your actions but also in relation to the steward's instructions. This consideration should also be extended to the advanced classes when your actions are related to stewards' instructions without being accompanied by commands.

If you halt or turn too quickly, you are likely to surprise your dog, resulting in a fault. If you spend too much time gathering your wits, as it were, you will be penalized for 'walking on'. It is generally accepted that a pace or two between the steward's instruction and the handler's reaction is the correct tolerance.

We have already stressed the importance of timing any Turn or Halt commands so as to give your dog sufficient time to react. Consider now the sequence of events when a third link in the chain of command (the trainer or steward) is introduced.

The stipulated manoeuvre is now communicated first from steward to handler and thence from handler to dog and all within two paces or so. It is very important, therefore, to give your dog the maximum time possible to hear and understand your command before you act. You cannot afford to waste time between the steward's (trainer's) instruction to you and translating it to the dog.

Here is what happens as a common fault in Beginners/Novice competition. The steward calls the instruction to the handler. If there is any delay between this and the handler commanding the dog, one or two paces have already been taken. Therefore, the handler must Turn or Halt as the command to the dog is given, risking surprising the dog, or command and take an additional pace, risking being penalized for walking on.

It is absolutely vital, therefore, that you cultivate the habit of reacting immediately to the steward's instruction with your command to your dog, so that you are then able to take the extra pace to give your dog that vital time to react correctly.

If you can discipline yourself to do this, it will pay dividends, both in Novice and later in the more senior classes, for by then you will have developed a resistance to allowing yourself to be rushed or browbeaten by the steward. If you watch any of the top handlers, what we are saying here will become self-evident.

Heel Free

Even in Beginners and Novice you will be required to carry out the Heelwork with your dog both on and off the lead. It is absolutely vital that by the time you begin to consider going lead free you have perfected your timing of commands so that your dog is used to receiving plenty of prior warning as to what you are about to do. Your voice is now your principal contact with your dog.

To begin with, only very short straight stretches should be attempted, preceded by a left-hand circle, with the lead being replaced regularly, particularly if there is any sign of the dog drifting wide. The graduation can also come via a very fine lead of cord or twine, attached to the collar, which is so light that the dog hardly knows whether it is attached or not.

Perfected deportment (footwork) is also essential, as it is this which will eventually take over in the higher classes as the means of maintaining maximum confidence and concentration in your dog. The most important thing of all is not to rush things. Don't attempt to go lead free until the correct Heelwork position, on lead, is so ingrained that the lead itself becomes superfluous.

Eventually, you should be able to drop into what we call 'Heelwork Mode' while you are out walking with your dog, and as soon as he notices, he should automatically fall into place beside you in the correct position. This should be the same instinctive reaction as Presenting to your Novice Recall position. This is achieved as much by play and praise in your left-hand circle as anything else.

Slow Pace and Fast Pace

In Classes B and C, your Heelwork is also tested at slow and fast paces. In Class B each change of pace commences from a Halt, so you have the facility, through the single command which you are permitted, to warn the dog what is expected of him, i.e. 'Timmy Heel' as you set off in normal. 'Timmy Steady' as you set off in slow, and 'Timmy Fast' as you set off in fast.

Changes of Pace on the Move

In Class C, however, you may be required to change from one pace to another on the move, i.e. without coming to a Halt. In this event you are not permitted any command or signal without incurring a penalty. In training you must practise changing pace as smoothly as possible, particularly fast into slow and vice versa.

Slow pace should by now be as well established in the general curriculum of work as normal. The problem with slow pace is that it can become boring for the dog. None the less, through play and praise between short lengths it should not be difficult to maintain attention, building gradually to longer unbroken stretches. The main secret is to maintain a smooth unbroken and regular pace, wobble free, and again practice without the dog is important. Also, you may well find that the more substantial footwear referred to in the Introduction helps you keep better balance than very light shoes or pumps.

Another thing to remember in slow pace is that your turns should be maintained at the same regular tempo as your forward paces. A keen dog may develop a tendency to anticipate the turns and to beat you round them; it is very easy, subconsciously to speed up yourself to cover this up.

Conversely, if you feel that your dog is losing concentration, the tendency to turn quickly yourself to recover attention, or to tuck him in on Lefts can develop without you realizing it. Either of these variations can be, and should be, interpreted as an extra command and be penalized accordingly. Remember, the dog must be taught to work to your pace rather than you adjusting and varying your pace to suit the dog's.

As far as fast pace is concerned, its introduction comes easily in your left-hand circle where you can build up gradually through slow/normal into fast, then break the exercise and play. From then on, to graduate to straight lines, ensure that to begin with you do long stretches unbroken by turns to build up the dog's confidence, often breaking to play by throwing out your playtoy in front for the dog to fetch. When you have full confidence in a straight line, you may begin to introduce turns beginning with Right, then About and finally Left, only graduating from one to the next when you are satisfied that the dog is fully confident. Although we are considering Advanced Heelwork, do not forget in training to use your Novice commands to tell your dog which way you are going to turn and – most important at fast pace – in plenty of time.

One of the most difficult things for many handlers is to relax at fast pace; any inhibitions which develop in your own actions soon relay themselves to the dog who translates them into apprehension in his own movements, resulting in the tendency to fall behind (lag). The moment you perceive that this is happening in training or even when you are competing in the ring, you must revert to encouragement, even if it means throwing marks away. There is always next week's show, and a fault like this, if allowed to establish itself through trying to 'hang on till the end of the test' will be very difficult to overcome.

If you are trying too hard, and your dog is very sensitive it will become very easy to set up unnecessary apprehension and you must avoid pressure by constant reversion to play and praise. If your dog, however, is of a more forceful personality, this is one area where he will take over if you let him. Observe both your dog and yourself carefully.

There only remains in the Heelwork exercise, the Advanced Sit, Stand and Down on the move, and these will be dealt with separately in one of the final chapters. The reasons for this will be explained therein.

Problems and Solutions

Having dealt with the more complex turns and the use which can be made of them to improve some of the simpler changes in direction, there are very few other problems in Heelwork which may require special attention, but this is an appropriate point to consider them.

Inattention

Like all problems, only more so in this case, prevention is better than cure. Inattention, or the reluctance to watch and concentrate on you, has almost certainly been caused by a combination of poor timing in the early days of basic Heelwork training – not praising in time when attention is first achieved and/or using too much hand contact to try to maintain it.

Once it has developed, this problem may never be fully ironed out; but all is not lost. You must avoid the temptation to try to manipulate your dog's head into the Watch position. You must use your voice only to praise when you do achieve a little of the required attention, and you must improve your timing when you do so. With this combination you may be surprised how much improvement in basic accuracy can be achieved, even if you do not achieve the more exciting style of Heelwork which you see and admire in others.

Lagging

This usually occurs in fast pace. It is probably induced by introducing fast pace into Heelwork too soon or not establishing confident long stretches before introducing turns.

To solve the problem, go back to the left-hand circle, building up gradually from normal into fast and breaking into play. Then practise long stretches with your playtoy, throwing it out in front for the dog to chase and pick up. The very worst thing you can do is to try to jerk your dog up from behind into the correct position.

Forward Work

The stronger, more exuberant dog can tend to take over in Heelwork. The slightly forward, looking backward and upward, 'come on let's get on with it' style of work can seem too good to be true to begin with, but things quickly go from bad to worse, and before you know it your dog is half a length in front of you.

Again, prevention is better than cure. The early position of the hands on the lead can be used gently to restrain the young dog who begins to take over. If the habit has been allowed to develop, however, it is most unlikely that you will cure it by constantly jerking your dog back. This usually winds the dog up even more. A calmer approach is more likely to have the desired effect. Stop periodically, turn, and put your dog quietly into the Down beside you before continuing.

It may also be possible to persuade the dog that he is lagging by being too quick for him out of the turns and jerking the lead to make the dog catch up; this is absolutely fatal in trying to make a slow dog quicker. As opposites can often be used to effect, this procedure could be used on an overkeen dog, but you must exercise great care. Otherwise, you may create the lagging habit.

CHAPTER 6

The Retrieve

The temptation to commence teaching Retrieve by encouraging the dog to chase after a moving article that you have thrown for him is difficult to resist. The dog is, by nature, a hunting animal and it should be easy to exploit the natural instinct of the 'chase' to pursue the dumb-bell. You should not give in to this temptation, however, and to see why let us examine the exercise in more detail.

The Exercise

Begin with the dog off the lead in the Sit at the handler's left side. On instruction from the steward, the handler commands the dog to 'Wait'. On instruction from the steward, the handler throws the article to be retrieved. When the article has come to rest, and on instruction from the steward, the handler commands the dog out to fetch the article. The dog should return with the article to the Present position. On instruction from the steward, the handler takes the article from the dog. On instruction from the steward, the handler commands the dog back to the Heel position.

In Beginners and Novice any number of commands or signals may be given to ensure compliance and the required accuracy at the various stages of the exercise. In Class A, only a single simultaneous command and signal may be given at each instruction from the steward, and in Classes B and C only a single command or signal may be given. In Classes A, B and C, the dog is expected to give up the article when it is reached for by the handler, without command.

In Beginners, Novice and Class A, the retrieve article is a dumb-bell; in Classes B and C the retrieve article is provided by the judge and will vary vastly from show to show.

Typical faults can be all those outlined in Novice Recall (*see* p. 23) plus other inaccuracies, such as anticipation of the Send command, running past the article, fumbled or double pick-up, dropping the article during the Return or at the handler's feet, or not releasing the article cleanly as the handler reaches for it.

Teaching the Exercise

Imagine that you have managed to achieve some semblance of a Retrieve by throwing a dumb-bell, encouraging your dog to chase it, and catching it on return before the dog has chance to spit it out. The next step is to send the dog out to fetch the dumb-bell after it has come to rest; at this point much of the excitement will be lost for the dog and sooner or later when he is instructed to fetch it, he will fail to respond. 'You threw it; you fetch it', is the easily imagined thought going through the dog's mind at this stage and from that moment you will never be able to rely on the dog in Retrieve again. Somehow you need to ensure that the dog will respond consistently and enthusiastically.

To begin with it may seem that there is a danger that you will put the dog off completely, for there is a certain discipline introduced and maintained during the teaching phase which is not present in any other aspects of our training. To compensate for this, it is most important that praise and reward are forthcoming in great measure at every step forward which is achieved. In Retrieve and in its progression into Scent, the dog should be

62

The 'Hold' command. Use your thumb and forefinger to encourage the dog to open his mouth.

Reach out to hold.

executing the exercise in order to please you and for the associated praise and reward, not just for the fun of it.

The first step is to teach the dog to hold the dumb-bell on command. We begin only when the young dog has gained a full set of adult teeth. It is a good idea at this early stage to have both hands free which can be achieved by sitting on a chair with the dog on a lead which is then tied around your knee.

Take the dumb-bell, and offer it to the dog with the command 'Hold'. Almost certainly the dog will not understand, and you will have to tease the mouth open. This is done by placing your fingers over or under the dog's muzzle

and pressing the loose surrounding skin in toward the teeth; as soon as the mouth opens, pop the dumb-bell quickly between the dog's teeth, praising generously. Ensure that the dog does not drop the dumb-bell by holding the loose skin under his jaw while continuing to praise and stroke his head.

Here again the three 'Ts' come into play. The firm commanding tone of 'Hold' must instantly be changed to bright and genuine praise the split second that the dog has complied. If the correct balance of love and respect between you has already been established, there should be no need for any great battle of wills. Make no mistake, however. You must not take

The dumb-bell is moved nearer to the ground, and the command 'Hold' is given.

'No' for an answer at any stage of the proceedings.

When your dog will take the dumb-bell on command, gradually lower it closer to the ground. Each time the dog takes the dumb-bell, call his name in the bright Recall tone and back off into the 'Come fore' Novice Recall position, all still on the lead.

Eventually the next major step comes when you place the dumb-bell on the floor in front of you. While the dog has been willing enough to reach out to take the dumb-bell from your hands, this will almost certainly be the next point of resistance which you have to overcome. It is vital that on the command 'Hold' the dog picks up the dumb-bell himself. It may be that you have to guide his lead downward

and apply the aid to open his mouth as previously described, but you must keep this applied until the dog has taken the dumb-bell into his mouth. You must not give in and pick up the dumb-bell and pop it into the dog's mouth yourself.

This is 'make or break' time, and if you give in at this point, all your previous efforts will have been in vain. Remember, however, that the split second when the dog has done what you wanted and picked up the dumb-bell, your praise should more than compensate for any pressure which may have been created.

Once the pick-up off the floor has been achieved, the finer points of the exercise can be addressed. With the dog still on the lead, the dumb-bell may be placed or dropped a yard

Pick-up from the ground. This may be the next major hurdle.

To encourage the dog to pick up while facing the handler, rather than picking up on his journey away from the handler, extend your left leg to make him first go round the dumb-bell before picking it up.

(metre) or so in front of you. On the command 'Hold', take the dog out with a pace forward with your left foot which is placed at the left side of the dumb-bell. Guide the dog well past the dumb-bell and then round so that he picks up the dumb-bell coming back towards you.

As soon as the dog has picked up the dumb-bell, call his name in your bright commanding Recall tone, and adopt the Novice Recall position which by now is irresistible to the dog. This procedure must be repeated countless times, still on the lead, until it is second nature to the dog to turn before picking up the dumb-bell; this will ensure that the first thing that he sees after the pick-up is you in your Novice Recall position. Coupled with the dog's name, this will ensure a smart and direct return.

Lead Off

When graduating to a lead-free Retrieve, the same procedure should be adopted with the dumb-bell dropped only a pace or two in front of you and you going out with the dog to ensure the turn before the pick-up. The length of throw can gradually be increased while your length of accompaniment out with the dog can be reduced, but if your dog shows any signs of picking the dumb-bell up 'on the run', before turning, you must revert to going out the full distance with him.

The Mark

It is very important at as early a stage as is possible to teach your dog to 'mark' where the Retrieve article has fallen. While you are using a clearly coloured dumb-bell, providing that the area is not too rough or congested, it will be easy for the dog to relocate it upon your

The Retrieve

Teaching the dog to mark the article. Hold the dog's head steady and throw the article a short distance; at the same time, give the command 'Look'.

Holding the mark.

Send command, even if he has looked away after it has landed. We spend so much time early in the dog's life teaching 'Watch me' that if we are not careful, this can work against us in Retrieve and, indeed, in Sendaway. We must, therefore, train the dog to 'mark' the Retrieve – to begin with as a separate exercise.

Hold the dog's head as shown in the photo, give the command 'Look', and throw your Retrieve article. Try to achieve plenty of height in the trajectory of the article and even guide your dog's head to follow it. If your dog will fix his gaze on where the article falls, even for a few seconds, break off and praise. Alternatively, ask a training companion to stand twenty to thirty paces away and drop an article while you hold your dog's head and encourage

him to mark by saying 'Look'. Again, if your dog will hold the 'mark' for a few seconds, break off and praise.

Once your dog has learned to look on command, it may be a good idea instead of saying 'Wait' or 'Sit' as your last command before throwing your article to use 'Look' as an encouragement to the dog to direct his eyes forward at the time that you throw your article.

Eventually the full Retrieve will be achieved, but in training always remember to use your dog's name just once on the pick-up; this will ensure that the reaction to look up to see you in your Novice Recall position becomes habit. When in the ring in Class A or above, of course you must stay silent but by this time the reaction to look up to see where you are on

Send your dog by giving the command 'Hold'.

Adopt the Novice Recall position. When the dumb-bell is clear of the ground, call the dog's name.

pick-up will have become so ingrained that the action will have happened before the dog has had a chance to miss the actual command.

As in Novice Recall, no further commands should be necessary until the Present is complete, at which time the praise should be such that this is the point in the exercise that the dog wants to get to as quickly as possible.

If you have any doubt at the last split second that your dog is going to Sit straight, take a pace or two backward and say 'Sit' on the move. Do not let your dog Present crooked and then correct it; even more so than in Novice Recall, you will have negated all the good work that the dog has already done, and all that he will retain from the exercise is the memory of being corrected for the last section.

As in Novice Recall, give the command 'Sit' just before the dog reaches you.

Graduating from the Dumb-Bell

The dumb-bell that you have been using should have been a reasonable size and colour (preferably white), to enable the dog's eyes to locate it quickly as soon as you send it. However, as the tests progress beyond Class A into Classes B and C the Retrieve articles are provided by the judge, and they will vary tremendously in size, shape, texture and colour. The only restriction placed on the judge by the rules is that the article should not be injurious to the dog. Glass, sharp metal, articles so small that they may be swallowed or so large that the dog is physically incapable of picking them up are therefore forbidden, but that leaves a huge variety of objects which the dog may be required to 'mark' and pick up. The more disciplined training programme described in the previous section will leave the dog more inclined to make the effort when the going gets tough.

It is important to graduate to other articles through a series of objects of ascending difficulty rather than plunging in at the deep end with a large, heavy metal article. Pieces of round wood or plastic similar to the shank of the dumb-bell are ideal.

Now that your dog has been taught the Retrieve, it does no harm to revert to play retrieves where the dog may be allowed to chase after the article as a game. This presents a good opportunity to introduce more unusual and different articles. Always remember that even when doing a fun retrieve, you should still call out your dog's name as soon as he has picked up the article, and adopt your Novice Recall position. Having done one or two play retrieves with your strange article you may then do a complete formal one, then perhaps another fun one to finish.

If you choose an article which is very difficult for the dog to carry, and a little pressure has built up during the completion of the exercise, always finish with another Retrieve on an easier article or your own familiar dumb-bell.

When taking a strange article for the first time ensure that you rub it thoroughly, so that your scent is left on it. This will give the dog more confidence to pick it up. If the article is an awkward shape, ensure that you handle it only at the centre or point of balance. This will encourage your dog to pick it up at the same point, so that it can be held in his mouth as easily as possible.

Basics to Remember

- Ensure your dog is sitting square, comfortably, at your left-hand side.
- Before indicating to the steward that you are ready, show your dog the article saying 'Hold it' or 'Fetch it' in an excited tone (of course you must not at this stage let your dog take hold of the article). Remember to handle the article properly and ensure it is thoroughly scented.
- Having been asked by the steward if you are ready and indicated that your are, await the instruction 'Command your dog' (Beginners or Novice), or 'Last command' (Class A or above).
- Give your dog your last command, i.e. 'Look', in a firm tone.
- Upon instruction from the steward, throw your article. Endeavour to gain sufficient height to gain the dog's interest while maintaining sufficient distance and accuracy.
- Upon instruction from the steward, send your dog by command 'Hold' or 'Fetch'.
- While your dog is on his way from you, adopt your Novice Recall position.
- In Beginners or Novice, and almost always in training, do not forget to give your dog's name in your bright commanding tone as soon as the dumb-bell is clear of the ground in your dog's mouth.
- In Beginners or Novice do not forget to say 'Sit' while your dog is still a yard (metre) or so away from you to encourage him into that position while there is still some forward impulsion.
- On instruction from the steward 'Take your article', do not be in too much of a hurry to comply. The tendency to snatch at the article will encourage the dog to drop it prematurely. Reach down slowly and take the article with both hands.

Problems and Solutions

Anticipation

It is quite common for dogs to anticipate the 'Send' command following a fairly disciplined course of training. Once the dog is absolutely sure what is required of him and any slight reluctance or apprehension has turned to confidence, the tendency to anticipate often crops up.

A simple cure is to have a training companion standing where the dumb-bell or article is going to land. Give your dog the Wait command, and throw your article. If your dog anticipates, you say nothing but your friend quickly and quietly picks up the article before the dog reaches it and returns it to you. Your dog will soon get the message.

You can even ask your friend to act as a steward and sing out 'Send your dog'. A dog that has developed the tendency to anticipate often reacts to the steward's command before you do. If so, your friend simply picks up the article and returns it. Soon you will be able to count to three or four after the 'Send your dog' instruction to ensure it is you that the dog is obeying and no one else.

Overrun

This is when the dog runs out far too quickly, picks up the article on the run, runs on, returns too quickly, and bumps into you on Present. This is what we call the 'nut case' Retriever. If the dog has been correctly trained through the disciplined Retrieve, this fault should not occur. It usually crops up as a result of a dog being play-trained or because he picked up the exercise so easily that you did not think that a disciplined progression was necessary.

The answer is to do only very short Retrieves in training, mostly on the lead, so that you can take the dog around the article to pick it up facing towards you rather than running on. Once it has been allowed to develop,

this fault can be extremely frustrating and very time-consuming to cure, but it can be done; a friend of ours had a Border Collie bitch who was one of the maddest Retrievers we have ever seen, but by persevering with the foregoing procedure, he eventually calmed her down sufficiently to turn her into a very much respected Obedience Champion.

Mouthing

'Mouthing' is often associated with over-running, but it can also occur in its own right, caused by not spending enough time in the early training of the exercise to teach the dog to hold securely. It can also be aggravated by the current Scent requirements, which are all now carried out on cloths. The dog does not hold the article securely but opens and closes his mouth intermittently upon it. Brittle articles are often cracked, and light articles, such as scent cloths, can be dropped.

The cure is to go back to basics and spend time at the dog's side insisting that he holds a variety of articles without mouthing. Pop them into the dog's mouth and take hold of the loose skin under his chin. Gradually, relax your hold, but regain it quickly and say 'Hold' quite firmly if the mouthing recurs. Praise when you feel you are making progress.

Slow Walk In

This is when the dog only walks out to the article and walks back showing little or no enthusiasm. It is usually caused by the wrong mixture of firmness and praise during training and too much verbal encouragement and direction while the dog is away from you. If you have overcorrected your dog for a crooked Present after completing a Retrieve, this will often take the shine off the main part of the exercise for him.

To improve, try to bring more enjoyment back into the exercise. Throw the article a fairly long way to give the dog time to build up a good pace both outward and on the return. Also, try to achieve plenty of height when you throw the article and encourage the dog to follow its trajectory. Finally, apart from your single bright Recall command on pick-up, try to remain silent until your dog has returned and Presented, so that he wants to get back quickly for praise.

Crooked Presents

If your dog Sits consistently crooked one side, *see* Chapter 1.

Hanging On

'Hanging on' is when the dog will not release the article when the handler reaches for it, but hangs on instead. This fault usually develops out of a play-training.

The worst thing you can do is to try to pull the dumb-bell or article out of the dog's mouth, as this simply perpetuates the game. Instead, simply put both forefingers on the bell or article and let them rest there. If the dog pulls away, call him back into the Present, and repeat the procedure. When he realizes that the game is over, he will soon learn to release when you reach out. In the meantime, if the problem persists at shows, as you reach to take the article, quickly insert both forefingers through the back corners of the dog's lips as a smooth action to persuade the dog's mouth open as you take the article.

Finish Anticipation

If the dog anticipates the Finish, it will be your own fault for practising it as part of the exercise instead of separately.

For a cure, *see* chapter 4.

CHAPTER 7

Class A Recall

Once you have won out of Novice, the Novice Recall ceases to be an exercise in its own right, although, as we have previously pointed out, it remains an important aspect of many of the Advanced progressions and should remain on the training curriculum throughout the dog's working life. What replaces it in the next class is the Class A Recall which in turn becomes the recall from Sendaway in Classes B and C.

The Exercise

Commence with the dog off the lead at the handler's left side. On instruction from the steward 'Last command', the handler commands the dog to Wait. As in Novice Recall, we use the command 'Wait' or 'Sit', reserving the command 'Stay' for the Stay exercises only.

Immediately following 'Last command', the handler is instructed by the steward to 'Leave your dog'. The handler moves forward alone and is directed by the steward along a predetermined route. This may include a number of turns and sometimes a Halt.

At a predetermined point, while still walking forward, the handler is instructed by the steward to 'Call your dog', at which time the handler commands the dog in to Heel. The dog must rejoin the handler smartly, then they continue forward together until instructed to Halt, when the dog should Sit at the handler's side without command. The exercise is concluded, and the dog released on instruction from the steward 'Exercise finished'.

The Recall from Sendaway (*see* chap. 9) in Classes B and C follows a similar pattern after the dog has been Downed at, or as near as

possible to, the designated place. From the steward's next instruction to the handler 'Forward' the same procedure will apply as from when leaving your dog.

Let us now consider the commands given to the dog. As in Retrieve the last command before leaving your dog may be a simultaneous command and signal. However, it may be worth developing reliance on only one or the other at this stage as you will only be able to use one or the other in any exercise in Classes B and C.

More important than this, however, is the consideration of your Recall command. In Class A a simultaneous command and signal can be given in addition to the dog's name. In the Recall from Sendaway in Classes B and C, however, the dog's name followed by only a command or a signal is permitted. Sometimes the habit of using both in Class A is difficult to break in Classes B and C. It is quite common to see handlers giving combined commands and signals on Recall from Sendaway, and in some cases they go unnoticed by the judge. However, they should be penalized.

The dog's name in your bright commanding Novice Recall tone should be sufficient to encourage your dog to come to you, particularly if this is reinforced by turning your head to look directly at your dog while you say it. This head movement can, and indeed should, be interpreted as your signal, but it also has the advantage that you can see if your dog has reacted and is on his way. In Class A, you can – if necessary – supplement your head signal with a quick command if you consider that the dog is slow to react, but we try to do without this as soon as possible, so that the Recall habit formed will carry us through to Classes B and C.

Remember also that if you have turned your head, that is your permitted signal used for Classes A, B and C. If in A you *also* use an arm signal, even if you do not take advantage of a verbal command, you may well be penalized; this is why our 'name and head signal only' procedure is best to adopt early.

Teaching the Exercise

Start with your dog on the lead at your left side. Hold the end of your lead in your left hand, slightly behind you so that there is plenty of slack. Tell your dog to 'Sit' or 'Wait', and step off with your right foot. As you come to the end of the lead, just before it becomes tight (timing is important here), turn your head to face your dog, call his name (using a bright commanding Recall tone), and pull gently on the lead to encourage your dog forward. Shorten the lead as your dog joins you, and continue forward in Heelwork mode for a few paces. Then break the exercise, and play. Do not come to a Halt. The distance travelled before you call your dog can now be increased by extending your lead length by clipping on a second lead to the metal ring on the loop end of the first. Do not forget to gather in this longer length of lead carefully after you have used it to get your dog on the move. Otherwise, it can easily become entangled in the dog's feet.

Continue with this procedure until you feel sure that your dog has learned what is required of him, and then try a short one off the lead – only three or four paces in a straight line, continuing forward in Heelwork mode in a straight line breaking into play after a few paces without coming to a Halt. When you have built up to a dozen or so paces before calling your dog you are ready to start to introduce a few turns but let the easiest come first.

After leaving your dog for a few paces, turn left and call immediately so that your dog joins you on the left-hand side. When your dog has joined you, continue for a few paces in Heelwork and break into play. Alternate this procedure by calling your dog and then turning left before he has rejoined you. (Ensure that the more enthusiastic type of dog does not bump into you by giving a firm 'Steady' command just before the point of impact.)

When the dog has become fully used to joining you on the left-hand side, it is time to introduce the rejoin after you have turned to the right.

As your right-hand side is now nearest the dog, the tendency for the young, inexperienced dog is to join you on that side and to continue Heelwork on the wrong side. We therefore commence by leaving the dog and calling while still walking in a straight line. By looking over your left shoulder as you call your dog, you can observe his progress as he catches you and turn right just as he does. Next time you can repeat the procedure, but turn right a pace or two before he catches you, maintaining encouragement over your left shoulder.

In our experience young dogs often do their best Heelwork just after they have joined their handlers in Class A Recalls. You can take advantage of this to turn it into a fun exercise, which will improve both the Recall side of things and your Heelwork off lead.

Basics to Remember
- Try to develop a single command or signal to Wait.
- Step off with your right foot.
- Call your dog by name only and use a head signal looking over your left shoulder, whichever side your dog will be coming from.
- Do not come to a Halt in training, but continue forward in Heelwork for a while.

Problems and Solutions

Anticipation

This is caused by calling your dog all the time, particularly as soon as you hear the steward's/trainer's instruction.

Do not always call your dog to Come. Once out of three, Return to the Heel position and praise. Also, on the steward's command, in training, get a quick 'Wait' command in or practise counting to three before calling.

Slow Rejoin

This is usually caused by coming to a halt (often because you have been instructed to do so) before your dog has caught up with you. Another cause is keeping your dog waiting too long while you are directed on a route march here there and everywhere.

To improve, revert to short Recalls, continuing forward in fun Heelwork, with lots of praise and breaking straight into play without a Halt.

CHAPTER 8

Scent Discrimination

We now come to possibly the most fascinating, frustrating, rewarding, heartbreaking, exciting aspects of dog work – Scent Discrimination. Notice we say dog work, rather than training, for we believe that Scent Discrimination is one thing that we must not delude ourselves into thinking that we can teach or train the dog to do. Here is a true story to help demonstrate what we mean.

When we had our first dog, Robbie, while he was still just a young pet, quite some time before we even knew that Obedience existed, we tried an experiment one day while we were playing with him; we put out a line of six empty matchboxes, making sure that they were only handled by someone else. Bron then picked one up, rubbed it, and put it back, making sure that Robbie did not see it, and then sent him to investigate. After a few inquisitive sniffs, the matchbox with Bron's scent on it was identified and picked up, and when he was called, Robbie carried it to her.

He had never been to training classes at that time, but Robbie was doing what was in those days a Class B Scent as a party trick; and it was achieved as a game by exploiting the dog's natural curiosity and sense of smell. What's more, he never failed.

The purpose of telling this story is to try to reinforce our philosophy and approach to this subject. A dog lives by his nose; his sense of smell is infinitely superior to ours, and yet we presume to teach the dog to do Scent.

Here, probably for the first time in our relationship with our dog, we find ourselves trying to take a dog through an exercise where he is

Basics to Remember

- Never, ever, correct your dog while he is working over the Scent articles. Particularly, never say 'No' if he picks up an incorrect article or cloth.
- Never send a dog out to do a second Scent in training or at a show. Right or wrong, you must accept the first attempt, praise, and walk away. The only distinction you should make between when the dog is correct and when he is wrong is that your praise should be far more exuberant when he is correct. A quiet 'Good lad' or 'Good girl' when the dog has failed compared with real excitement and praise when he is correct will provide the required contrast between right and wrong without creating the apprehension and fear of being corrected which can be the downfall of so many (yes, we have been there as well).
- Never try to force a dog to 'take Scent'. If in Class A or B, your dog has to find a cloth with your scent on it. He already knows full well what you smell like, so there is no need to rub your hand all over his nose. A light brush over, accompanied by an excited 'Find it' will be sufficient. If in Class C, your dog has to take an unfamiliar scent and memorize it. He will more readily do this as a fun, inquisitive response if you don't thrust the cloth against his nose.
- At all stages of Scent training, you must ensure that all 'blank' articles and cloths remain absolutely untainted by your own scent. This is not as easy as it may sound as your dog's nose is so sensitive that the slightest touch or even indirect contact with some other items handled by you can 'contaminate' your blanks, causing confusion in your dog's mind. You would be wise to enlist the help of a friend, husband, wife, etc. when laying out scent patterns, so that you can be sure that only the correct article or cloth has your (or the judge's) scent on it.

the expert, and we are mere hangers on. If we can recognize, accept, and exploit this superior expertise without rancour, the dog will be proud as well as confident. If we try to take over and know best, to correct or even chastise the dog when we think he is wrong, he will lose confidence more quickly and more irrevocably than in any other exercise.

The Exercise

At all levels, Scent contains all the requirements of a good Retrieve. There is more to it, of course, but a good reliable and accurate Retrieve is a prerequisite. All the rules concerning commands, signals, etc., for each level, which apply to Retrieve, apply equally to Scent. Markable faults and inaccuracies in Novice Recall and Retrieve are the same in Scent. However, extra commands while the dog is working the Scent area usually result in the forfeit of all allocated marks for that exercise. If the dog pecks at, or mouths, an incorrect cloth or decoy, marks will be deducted, even if the correct cloth is eventually returned. If the correct cloth is selected but put down again or dropped on the way back this will also be penalized.

These days Scent Discrimination in all classes – A, B and C – is carried out on cloths, that is cloth material squares not less than 6in (18cm) but not more than 10in (25cm) square. All cloths should be slightly weighted in some way to prevent them blowing away in windy conditions.

In Class A, five cloths are laid out in a straight line pointing directly in front of the handler. All cloths are 'blank', that is to say they exhibit nothing but their own natural scent and should not be touched directly by hand. Amongst these cloths is placed a further cloth, which has been held by the dog's handler. It is placed in the same position in the line for each competitor in the class.

The dog must not be allowed to see the cloth being placed, but when it is in position, the dog is brought into the Heel position by the handler, who may then provide whatever instruction he believes necessary to tell the dog what is required of him (setting up).

On instruction from the steward 'Last command', the handler must tell the dog to Wait. The dog must not be sent to find the correct cloth until the steward instructs the handler to do so. After being commanded out by the handler, the dog should discriminate between the unscented cloths, identify the one with his handler's scent on it, and return with it as per Retrieve, including Present and Finish.

In Class B, as you would expect, the exercise becomes more demanding. Nine cloths are laid out in a random pattern, and a decoy is introduced; that is to say one of the cloths is handled by another person so that there is now another scent, which the dog must discriminate against. A tenth cloth, which has been scented by the handler, is placed into the pattern, and the procedure is repeated as for Class A.

In Class C the whole exercise advances dramatically, for at this point the handler's scent is abandoned completely. Up to ten cloths are laid out in any pattern. At least two decoys are included, using the same person or two different ones. The scent which the dog is required to find is the judge's. For each dog, the judge handles two cloths, one of which is laid out in the scent pattern while the dog is turned away. The other cloth is then given to the handler who presents it to the dog in order that he memorizes the scent. This is known as 'giving the dog scent', and requires the dog to 'take scent'. It is a very important part of the exercise.

The handler must again stand up straight, clear of the dog, before receiving the steward's instruction to 'Send your dog', upon which the dog is commanded out by the handler to find and return with the judge's scent cloth, rejecting the decoys on the way if they are encountered first.

Developing the Exercise

While it is not for us to presume to teach Scent, we do have to manipulate the dog's best attribute, without pressure, into the same finely tuned accuracy that is the basis of all the Obedience curriculum. Until fairly recently, cloths were not used except for Class C, and in Class A scent was carried out over a number of random articles with the correct article being a familiar one provided by the handler.

The 'progression' to the current more disciplined type of Scent at this level was, in our opinion, one of the most retrograde steps we have seen in all our years in Obedience and one which we were strongly against at the time. Most of the people who were instrumental in this change had very little 'grass roots' involvement in working dogs in Obedience, and many more, to their eventual regret, were rather apathetic at the time. However, we are now stuck with cloth scents at all levels, so we have to make the most of it.

The dog's introduction to the exercise should be through the sequence which we always apply. We begin by using the dog's playtoy, which is preferably the knotted cloth referred to in chapter 1, as the Scent article. We throw it out amongst five or six large, immovable objects. We even let the dog see it fall at first. This is, of course, a simple Retrieve to begin with, the idea being merely to get the dog accustomed to bringing back something from among other articles. Remember, even at this early stage, as your dog leaves you, adopt your Novice Recall position. Immediately the dog has lifted the article clear of the ground, call his name in your bright commanding Recall tone. Nothing more should be said until your dog has Presented, when praise is in order as usual.

The next stage is to turn your dog away or cover his eyes while the article is placed amongst others. Then let him face the articles and say 'Find it' with your excited encouraging tone of voice. Having done several Retrieves amongst the articles, the dog should by now,

on command (choose one word only, and stick to it: 'Find', 'Seek', or 'Fetch'), set out to bring in his playtoy. As soon as the article is in the dog's mouth, call his name once and once only as for Novice Recall, with you in the correct position. You may now graduate to placing the playtoy amongst smaller varied articles, though none of them should be more tempting than the dog's own article.

If your Playtoy/Scent article up to now has not been a knotted cloth, now is the time to introduce one. It is worth spending some time encouraging your dog to hold it without mouthing. Again, at first the dog may see the cloth thrown into the articles before it is placed in a more formal way. Again, the same Novice Recall/Retrieve posture and command should be retained.

When the dog is fully confident to explore the articles to find his knotted cloth, it can then be undone and laid out as a square though still amongst different articles. The dog is still recognizing his own familiar article.

At the same time, you can begin introducing a Scent amongst similar articles, one of which can be used first as a Retrieve. The remaining articles should be made difficult or even impossible to pick up. Take, for instance, six cardboard toilet roll tubes. Fill five of them up with sand/cement so that they are quite heavy. After a few Retrieves with the empty one, throw it amongst the others and send your dog to fetch it. Next, you can place the empty tube amongst the others without the dog seeing. This can be quite a fun exercise, but you are at last achieving a true discrimination on scent, while still ensuring as much as possible that the dog cannot go wrong.

Hiding the Playtoy

Another way to encourage and give the dog confidence to use his nose is to make up four or five cardboard 'tents' by folding pieces of cardboard about 12in × 8in (30cm × 20cm) in half so they can stand on the floor and pro-

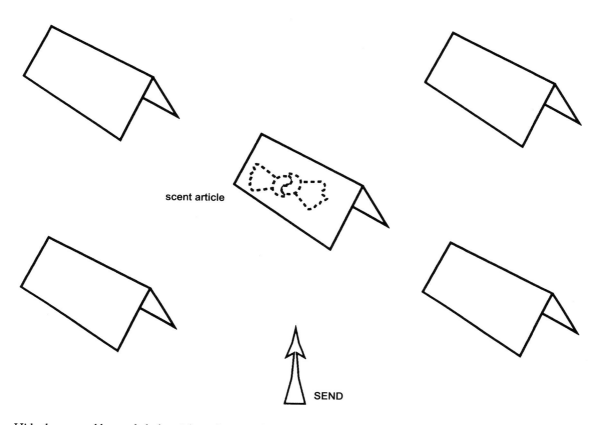

scent article

SEND

Hide the scented knotted cloth article under one of the cardboard tents.

vide a place to hide your knotted cloth. Arrange your tents into a pattern over an area of 2½–3½yd² (2–3m²), take your dog a few yards (metres) away, and tell him to Wait. Take your cloth/playtoy and pretend to put it under one and then another tent. Put it under the third or fourth one, and return to your dog. Using your excited tone of voice, tell your dog to 'Find it', and send him out to explore the tents. This can be very much in the form of a game, but all the time the dog is gaining confidence in using his nose.

Graduating to Cloths

You can now begin to turn your attention to the more formal Scents which will have to be executed in the ring, but you should still pursue a policy of trying to ensure as far as is possible that the dog can not make a mistake.

Our first idea for doing this was to take a long piece of string and tie half a dozen cloths along it at about 2½ft (75cm) intervals. The ends of the string can be pegged down so that your own cloth, knotted or undone, can be thrown or placed along the line. When your dog is sent out to find it, any mistakes in the shape of the dog pecking at or attempting to pick up a neutral cloth will be quickly negated without any correction from yourself. You must, of course, find a training friend to handle and put out the cloths, as you have to avoid even the slightest contact with the cloths at all costs.

These days we use another set-up to main-

77

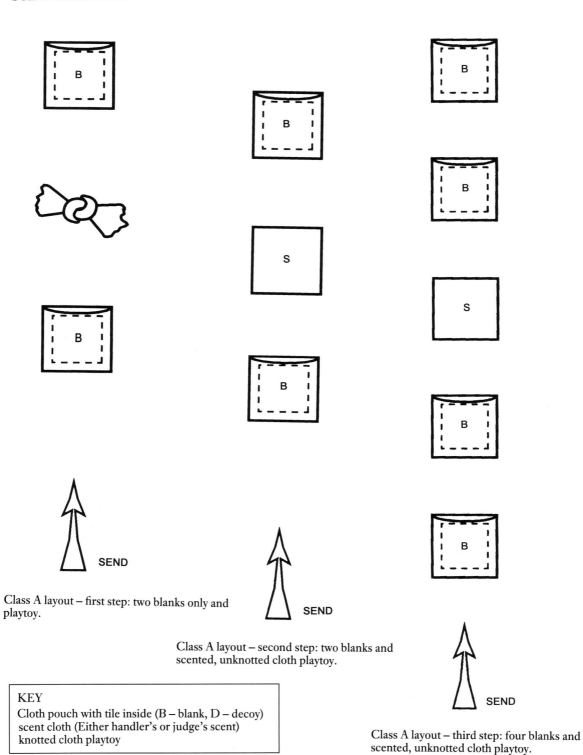

Class A layout – first step: two blanks only and playtoy.

Class A layout – second step: two blanks and scented, unknotted cloth playtoy.

KEY
Cloth pouch with tile inside (B – blank, D – decoy)
scent cloth (Either handler's or judge's scent)
knotted cloth playtoy

Class A layout – third step: four blanks and scented, unknotted cloth playtoy.

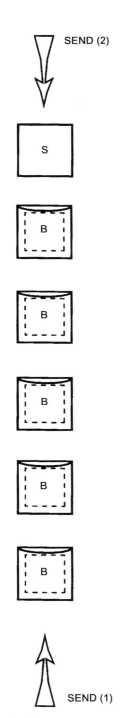

Class A layout – fourth step: five blanks and scented, unknotted cloth playtoy at end. Send dog from each end alternatively.

tain the same philosophy. We have a set of a dozen or so cloth pouches approximately 8in (20cm) square into which can be inserted a heavy tile or even a steel plate. They can be placed out anywhere indoors or out, and when the young inexperienced dog tries to pick them up, they have the same effect of light discouragement without pressure or commands from the handler. Thus, the dog goes on to explore further until he comes to the correctly scented cloth.

Now you can progress through to a simple straight line Class A Scent without a decoy. Begin with only two blanks plus the handler's cloth, and build up gradually to the maximum of six cloths. Then move to a more complex layout in Class B with one or two of the cloth pouches containing a tile handled by a separate person to provide decoys.

Throughout this progression, your dog is still only searching for the cloth with your own familiar scent on it. As we said previously, it is hardly necessary to remind him what you smell like, and the habit that has developed amongst handlers of rubbing their hands all over the dog's nose is unnecessary and irritating. Our 'set-up' at this stage involves just the lightest touch on the dog's nose with our fingers as we say in our excited tone of voice 'Find it'.

Graduating to Class C Scent

Eventually you will come to a major advancement when you leave Class B and move into Class C, for in this class, it is not your scent that your dog has to look for, but that of the judge. This is an enormous step for you and your dog because there is a very significant change not only in what goes on while your dog is working over the cloths but also – and probably more fundamentally – what goes on while you are setting your dog up before he is sent out.

Before you can expect your dog to find a strange scent, you must consider carefully how to place the memory of that scent into the

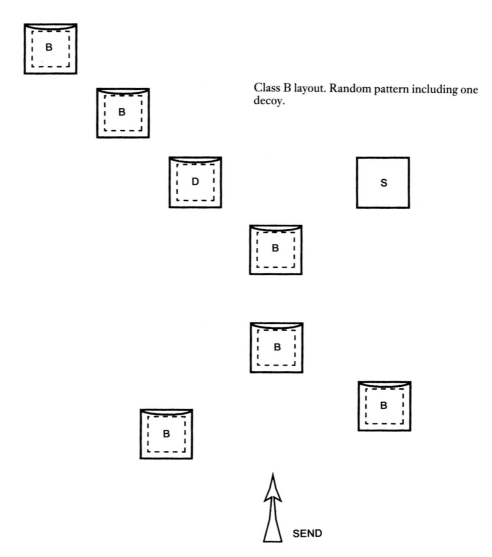

Class B layout. Random pattern including one decoy.

SEND

dog's brain — what is known as persuading the dog to 'take scent' — so that he can carry it with him, discriminate over decoys, and identify and return with the correct cloth.

To do this you must exploit the dog's natural sense of curiosity, which he expresses through the use of his nose, so that he takes scent naturally. When offered a scent cloth or any other strange article in a casual, relaxed way, the dog's first reaction is invariably to reach forward to take a sniff; in doing this, the dog has taken scent. If, in Class A and Class

B, you have insisted on rubbing your hand all over the dog's nose, and now for Class C you continue to do a similar thing by holding a cloth over the dog's nose, it would be little wonder if he has by now become resentful of the whole proceedings and is, therefore, far less likely to take and retain a strange scent with any real enthusiasm. One of the main factors in achieving a reliable Class C scent then is the art of encouraging the dog really to take scent.

To do this, simply call your dog up into the Present position with the scented cloth hanging from your hands in front of you. Providing that the dog takes only one small sniff at the cloth, this should be sufficient. It can be consolidated, however, when the dog is returned to the Heel position by again offering the cloth to the dog, still without pressure. The dog will even Sit and allow the cloth to be gently draped over his nose providing no pressure is exerted.

If Scent has been carried out as a pressure-free exercise up to this level and the stranger's

scent is offered as described, we invariably find that the first Class C scent that we ask the dog to attempt is carried out successfully.

In training, of course, we still use our cloth pouches and tiles for blanks and decoys, but even the first one or two Class C Scents attempted at shows are usually completed correctly. Problems begin to occur when your dog is asked to attempt too many Class C Scents. You may, for instance, go to one or two training clubs during the week where you practise a Class C scent or do one or two at home. You may then attend a show on Saturday and Sunday where you also have two Class C Scents.

If you have graduated to Championship status, you could even find yourself asking your dog to attempt two Class C Scents on both days. Almost before you know it, your dog may be attempting half a dozen Class C Scents in a week – that is six scents to remember and

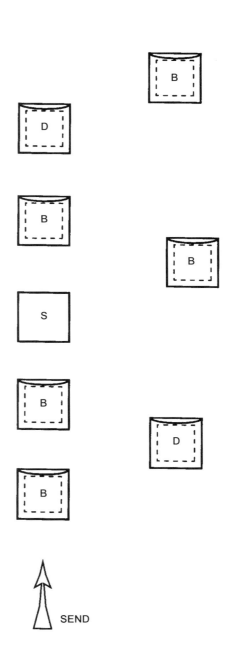

Class C layout. Random pattern including two decoys. During a test, the article to be retrieved will carry the judge's scent, but in training it should carry either your own or a very familiar scent.

twelve decoys to reject. This is when the confusion and the resulting apprehension can set in, particularly if the dog fails one or two and is corrected for them.

To maintain the dog's confidence, we find that it is better in training to go back on a regular basis to Class B Scents over decoys, practising a Class C Scent only rarely. Similarly, we would not attempt a Class C Scent at a show unless our dog was on a sufficiently good mark after the main work to be in with a chance of a place in the first six. An alternative to practising Class B Scents might be to practise a Class C Scent, but use another familiar and regular 'judge's scent'. This could be, for instance, your wife's or husband's. Although the dog is carrying out a Class C Scent, he is looking for something familiar and consistent. In this way, confidence is retained for when the odd 'real' Class C Scent is attempted.

One further observation we have made over the years and which we have turned to good use is in connection with the way the judge's scent cloth is held by the handler when giving the dog the Scent. Some people hold the cloth very carefully by the corners so as not to contaminate it with their own scent. We do not believe that this is important. Indeed, it can be more beneficial if some of your own scent does find its way on to the cloth. If the dog takes a mixture of the judge's scent and your own, when he is examining the cloths, the decoys should remain totally unfamiliar whilst the judge's scent is not only recognized in its own right but also 'feels' more familiar to your dog because it is associated with your own. This can be a great confidence booster.

We have made much of giving the dog the benefit of the doubt in Scent, and this applies particularly if the dog returns with a decoy in Class C. The basis of the exercise is the presupposition that every human scent is different – as individual as fingerprints – and this is undoubtedly the fact. None the less, taking, remembering, and matching scent for the dog can be likened to us matching colours from a large commercial paint colour chart where the various shades can be almost impossible to distinguish. Although every human scent is different, surely somewhere amongst the billions of people in the world very similar scents can be encountered. If the correct scent was green, and the decoy was blue, there would be no problem, but if the correct scent and decoy scent are only one subtle shade of green apart, and the dog hits the decoy first, the mistake, if he picks it up, is much easier to understand and sympathise with. Try to remember this analogy when you are tempted to correct your dog or send him out again if he has returned with the decoy.

CHAPTER 9

The Sendaway

Over the years the Sendaway has probably attracted more controversy than any other exercise in the Obedience curriculum. Looking at what is required it soon becomes easy to see why.

The Exercise

Commencing with the dog sitting at heel, the dog may be 'set up' by the handler who must then stand up straight, clear of the dog before receiving further instruction from the steward. Upon the next instruction from the steward 'Send your dog', the dog is commanded by the handler by word, signal, or both if they are simultaneous, away in the direction indicated by the judge. (It is these last six words which have led to the variation in interpretation of the rules and resulting controversy).

Upon reaching the designated point, the dog is commanded down by the handler. Upon command from the steward, the handler sets off along a designated route guided by the steward, during which – at the same point for each competitor – the handler is instructed to call the dog. The Recall from that point is the same as that described for a Class A Recall (see chap. 7).

The way that faults may occur is perhaps best left for the moment, for they all form part of the varied view and opinion on the exercise. We would not wish, however, to create the impression that we think more standardization should be introduced; we believe that there is scope in this exercise – within the rules – for enough variation to keep us all on our toes and test ourselves as trainers.

What it all comes down to is this: what does 'in the direction indicated by the judge' mean? Should this be interpreted as a point of the finger in the general direction of a clump of dandelions, or should the target be so clearly marked that the Sendaway becomes a 'Send to'?

In order to progress forward in a straight line, every animal, including the human being, needs a point of reference on which, consciously or subconsciously, to focus. This is why in a barren landscape such as a desert, it is all too easy to walk round in circles.

We try to bear this in mind when we train and compete with our dogs, and when we judge other people. Do we provide a consistent and easily recognizable point of reference, or do we leave it to the dog to select his own? The latter is not as unreasonable as some people think, as in the parallel sport of Working Trials, many of the top exponents are able to train their dogs to do just that, achieving Sendaways of several hundred yards (metres) to nothing more than 'that oak tree on the other side of the field' or similar.

There is, however, a fundamental difference between a Working Trials scenario and that at an Obedience Show. Working Trials tend to take place in relatively isolated locations where visitors and spectators are few and far between. The scene changes little throughout the day. At an Obedience Show you will find anything between ten and twenty rings set up with perhaps five hundred to a thousand people moving around. The scene outside the ring ropes is changing constantly with distractions and potential targets, which may or may not attract your dog, coming and going all day. A brightly coloured holdall or someone in a pair of white slacks carelessly positioned one minute can be gone the next; a wide variety of constantly changing attractions or distractions can be encountered.

A more specifically referenced type of Sendaway 'marker' has, therefore, evolved over the years, although the size, shape, number and arrangement can still vary enormously. Because the Sendaway has become, arguably, easier as a result, finer points of distinction in marking have also developed. The very slightest signs of deviation, hesitation or anticipation will be penalized. Although the variation in Sendaway markers is endless, their arrangement can be broadly categorized as follows:

1. Four markers, the dog being required to be Downed within the rectangle formed by an imaginary line around them.
2. A flat marker, such as a mat or four tapes or battens laid flat on the ground to form a rectangle, the dog being required to be Downed within the rectangle or on the mat.
3. A pair of markers with a further central marker some distance beyond, with the dog being required to be Downed a minimum distance beyond the first two markers or upon reaching the third.
4. A single marker with the dog being required to be Downed within a prescribed distance from it.

All these variations have a different degree of 'Send to' element to them, and all of them have varying degrees of likelihood to create some tendency in the dog to 'put the brakes on' of his own accord.

There is one more variation, which we believe is the best compromise, and this is to have two markers only, with the requirement for the dog to run through them a minimum distance (say 2–3yd (2–3m)), after which the dog may run on further without penalty providing that he does not deviate and Downs immediately on command. With this format there is nothing to encourage the dog to stop prematurely (unless he has not been trained properly) so that a good confident Sendaway can be demonstrated, while at the same time two good points of reference can be maintained to counteract the many distractions outside the ring throughout the day.

At this point it may be best to demonstrate how we set up and judge Sendaway before proceeding with the teaching of the exercise.

In the diagrams we show how our Sendaways are set up, with a few typical combinations of how the exercise might be marked. It can be seen that failure to make the distance is considered a greater fault than minor deviations from a straight line. Other inaccuracies stemming from overkeenness are penalized but less heavily than those arising from lack of impulsion.

One other point we would like to make before moving on to the teaching of the exercise concerns the choice of markers, or rather the choice of their colour. As we stated earlier, although we have our own very fixed ideas on the exercise, we would not wish to see it standardized more than it already is, and our training does try to take into account other people's ideas. However, if markers are used in any arrangement, careful consideration should be given to their colour.

First thoughts are that white is the best choice, and under some conditions, this colour does stand out, but you will also find that this is not consistently so. White markers with the sun shining from behind the set-up point will stand out very well, whilst later in the day when the sun is behind them they will become almost invisible. Similarly, if the sun is behind them, making them difficult to see, and a cloud passes over the sun, they will suddenly become much more obvious resulting in inconsistencies in the degree of visibility, resulting in some

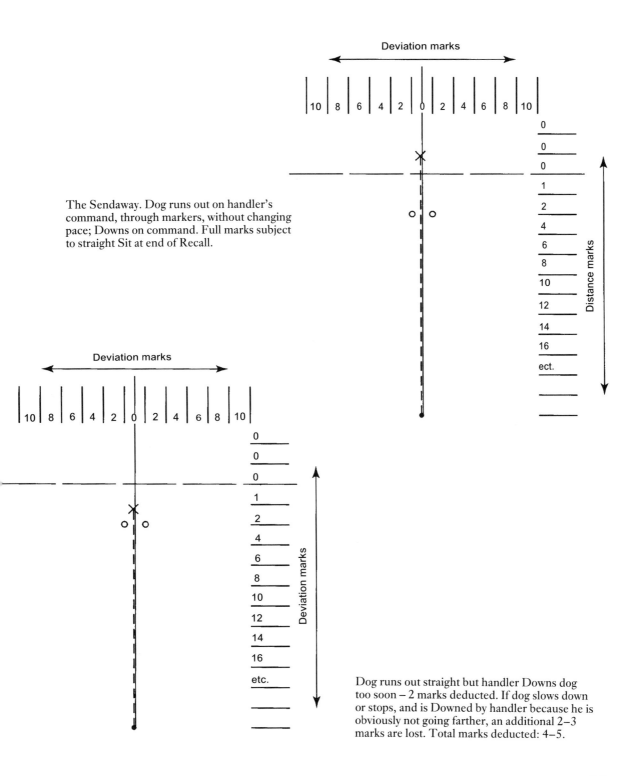

The Sendaway. Dog runs out on handler's command, through markers, without changing pace; Downs on command. Full marks subject to straight Sit at end of Recall.

Dog runs out straight but handler Downs dog too soon – 2 marks deducted. If dog slows down or stops, and is Downed by handler because he is obviously not going farther, an additional 2–3 marks are lost. Total marks deducted: 4–5.

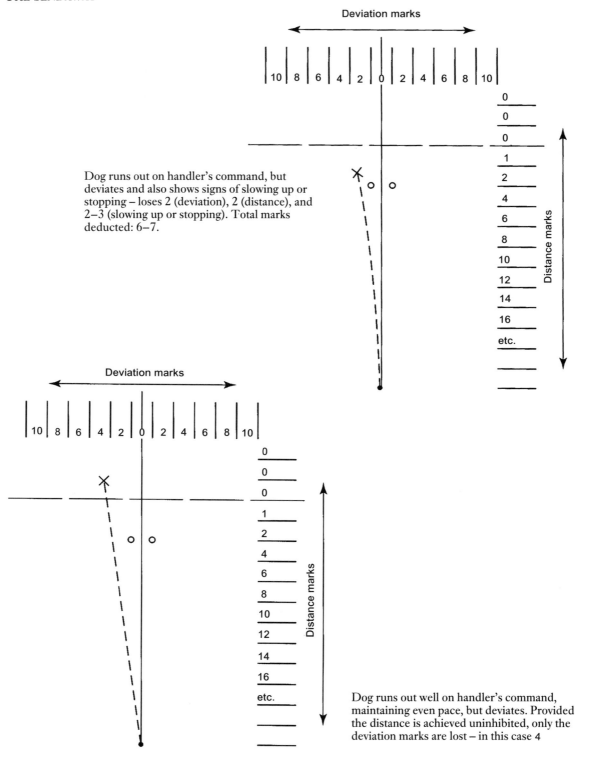

Dog runs out on handler's command, but deviates and also shows signs of slowing up or stopping – loses 2 (deviation), 2 (distance), and 2–3 (slowing up or stopping). Total marks deducted: 6–7.

Dog runs out well on handler's command, maintaining even pace, but deviates. Provided the distance is achieved uninhibited, only the deviation marks are lost – in this case 4

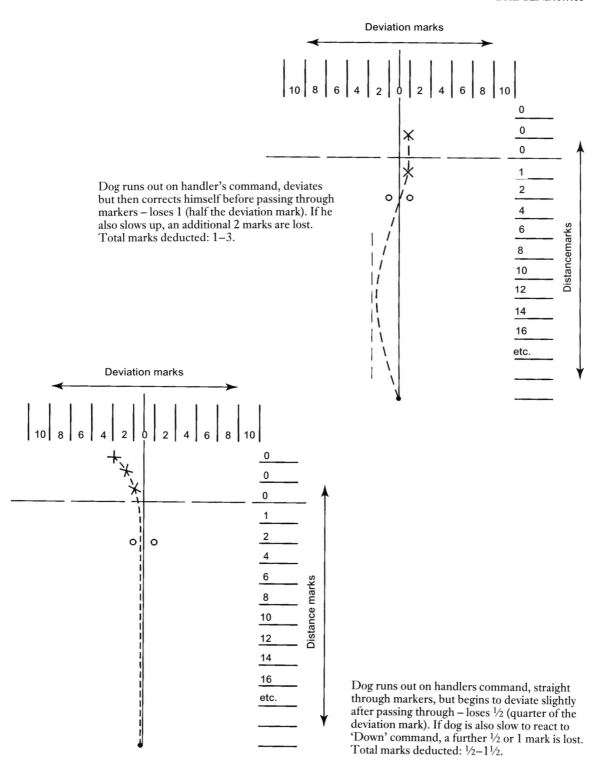

Deviation marks

|10| 8 | 6 | 4 | 2 | 0 | 2 | 4 | 6 | 8 | 10|

0
0
0
1
2
4
6
8
10
12
14
16
etc.

Distancemarks

Dog runs out on handler's command, deviates but then corrects himself before passing through markers – loses 1 (half the deviation mark). If he also slows up, an additional 2 marks are lost. Total marks deducted: 1–3.

Deviation marks

|10| 8 | 6 | 4 | 2 | 0 | 2 | 4 | 6 | 8 | 10|

0
0
0
1
2
4
6
8
10
12
14
16
etc.

Distance marks

Dog runs out on handlers command, straight through markers, but begins to deviate slightly after passing through – loses ½ (quarter of the deviation mark). If dog is also slow to react to 'Down' command, a further ½ or 1 mark is lost. Total marks deducted: ½–1½.

87

variation in the test for different dogs throughout the day.

The rules specifically require that the test remains the same for each dog, which is why we agree with the use of markers in the first place. If black or dark-coloured markers are used, it will be seen that variations in light or sun position have the least effect on their visibility, and the consistency of the test is maintained.

Teaching the Exercise

There are three essential ingredients to a good Sendaway. The first is an instantaneous Down. The second is that, when commanded, the dog looks straight and 'holds his mark'. That is, he selects a point on which to focus his gaze and holds that gaze. The last essential component is the zeal, speed, and energy in the Send itself that comes from the confidence of having no inhibitions in passing through markers.

The Instant Down

It is vital that your dog responds instantly to the Down command. Quite apart from competitive Obedience, it is probably the most practical thing you will ever teach your dog. In almost any sort of emergency, if your dog will Down on command and stay where he drops with confidence until you get to him, you should be able to avoid any serious mishaps. We teach our young dogs, while out for a walk on a lead, by giving the command and applying the aid as illustrated on page 30.

In a very short while, however, if we do not get an instant response, the aid is applied very quickly and quite forcefully. The praise which follows should prevent any serious inhibitions being created but you must never take 'No' for an answer.

If you say 'Down', the dog should respond unquestioningly, and if he does not, you have every right to get a little cross. There are any number of situations we can imagine where an

instant Down could save your dog's life; a little early confrontation, if followed up with the appropriate praise when you have achieved what you want, will be a very sound investment.

Look Straight

We have already stressed the importance in Retrieve of teaching the dog to mark where the article falls. This can be extended to Sendaway by setting up two markers and throwing an easily visible article between them, holding the dog's head forward and saying 'Look straight'. If your dog will hold the mark for a few seconds without looking back up at you, break the exercise and praise your dog.

Another method of teaching the dog to look straight is to set up two markers *with plenty of*

Look Straight

Teaching the command 'Look straight'.

distance behind them up to a tree or fence. Take some string, tie a piece of cloth to one end, pass the string through a wire of the fence or a nail in the tree and place the cloth in front of the markers with the string passing through them back to the nail or wire. Set the dog up holding his head forward and say 'Look straight', while drawing the cloth away from you through the markers by pulling the string. The idea is to teach the dog to hold the mark and to hold the 'Look straight' – not to send the dog to 'chase' the cloth. Again, if he holds his mark position for a few seconds, break off and praise.

Having spent so much time with your dog at your left-hand side teaching 'Watch me', you may find, in spite of all the foregoing methods, that he can not resist the temptation to look away from the markers as you stand up

Holding the Look straight, without any further direct help from the handler.

straight, and to look back up at you. If this is the case, begin again all the 'Look straight' procedures with your dog on your right-hand side so that he does not associate this with Heelwork attention. When you have established a 'Look straight' with your dog on your right-hand side, you can gradually move round the back of your dog while maintaining this attitude until you have it established with you in the correct position at his right side.

Eventually you should be able to stand with your dog at the Sit beside you, and on the command 'Watch me' the dog looks up to watch; on the command 'Look straight', the dog does just that – all as a self-contained, pressure-free exercise which does not have to include the Send until you need it in the ring.

The Send

The actual Send must come from the dog having confidence to be away from you, so you should begin training with familiar markers in a familiar place, using a well-known article like a piece of carpet or mat or playtoy.

Your youngster should first become used to being tied up in a familiar spot on his mat or with his playtoy – in the garden or at the end of the hall, or the same place at the club, while you carry on with some other task or conversation at a distance. You should avoid having your dog with you all the time at a club or at shows. He should become used to being tied up away from you (for short periods at first), gaining confidence from your frequent returns, until he feels secure in the knowledge that even though you are not with him you are never far away.

When the dog has become completely used to being in a familiar place, leave the playtoy or mat there, place two markers in front, and with your dog on the lead tell him to 'Look straight'. Pointing his head in the right direction, say 'Away', and run with him through the markers. Say 'Down' on the mat, and praise. This little game repeated often enough will soon result in the dog pulling you out on the

The Send. When first beginning training for this exercise, you need not stand up straight.

lead, and this is the first step in building up the necessary speed and confidence.

At the same time another phase of the 'Send' to begin to introduce is to set up your two markers. Still in your familiar area, with your mat behind, walk back across to the other side of the room or lawn and set the dog up as for Novice Recall but now you can practise your 'Look straight'. It does not matter if you have not got this perfected at this stage, but tell your dog to Sit and Wait, and walk away through the markers to the mat or playtoy.

The idea is to call the dog through the markers, but this time avoid your Novice Recall posture. Rather position yourself sideways-on and after using your dog's name to instigate the Recall, follow it with your 'Away' command. When your dog reaches you, give your 'Down' command, and apply the aid if necessary (by now your dog should be well used to a good firm Down command without taking

offence and should respond instantly without any further ado).

Quietly praise your dog in the Down position, tell him to 'Wait', and walk back through the markers. After a dozen or so paces, call your dog so that he passes through them as per Class A Recall. In this way your dog becomes thoroughly used to passing through the markers without stopping. Your dog will soon begin to associate the 'Away' command with running out to a familiar article in familiar surroundings. The next step is to take your familiar article (the mat) to less familiar surroundings – the park or the local recreation ground for instance – at which time the whole procedure is started again. Call your dog through the markers onto the mat several times before attempting the Send.

The location and type of marker can now be varied until your dog becomes used to doing the Sendaway in unfamiliar places through unfamiliar markers, but always begin with your familiar mat to give confidence. Even at shows, we always try to practise a Sendaway before we work in the ring. We carry a variety of markers which can be adapted to match as near as possible those being used by the judge; we also use our familiar article first to boost confidence.

We never do a Sendaway 'cold', i.e. without doing the call through first. An experienced, correctly trained dog should, of course, execute a good Sendaway without all this preparatory ritual at a show, but we still believe in giving the dog the very best chance.

You will find many of the other variations of Sendaway marker outlined earlier, but if you have a dog that will run on through markers and Down instantly on command, you should be able to adapt the training we have outlined so that you can stop your dog within four markers or on a mat, or let him run through markers up to a third. Remember, though, that you must never settle for second-best; if you allow your dog to stop when he thinks he has gone far enough and say 'Down' even though you know in your heart he was already going Down anyway, you will be creating a bad habit

The Sendaway

The Sendaway target. Note the abundance of space beyond.

Give the command 'Down' at least 3yd (3m) through the markers.

which will be almost impossible to break. At the first sign of an anticipated Down, even in the ring, you must straight away revert to calling through the markers and insisting on your dog running on until you say 'Down'.

In order to consolidate this, it is a good idea occasionally not to give the Down command at all, but when you are satisfied that your dog is running on well, simply recall and praise.

Basics to Remember

- Avoid, where possible, doing a Sendaway cold. Always practise one first in training by calling through. At the show try to set up a Sendaway as similar as possible to the one that you will be attempting in the ring and call through first before sending.
- Teach 'Look straight' as a separate exercise. Never send your dog unless he is looking straight.
- Do not point your finger toward the Sendaway when setting up your dog; this is a human convention that the dog will not understand. All that will happen is that the dog will look at your hand, not in the direction you wish him to.

- In training always set your Sendaway up so that there are no obstructions immediately behind the markers. Ideally there should be at least 20–30yd (20–30m) of unrestricted space beyond the markers. Never send your dog up to a hedge, fence, or wall.
- Never settle for second-best. Do not say 'Down' because you know your dog is going to do that anyway. If your dog anticipates the Down prematurely, revert back to basics by calling your dog through.
- Do not always Down your dog. If he has gone as far as you wish, just recall and praise.
- Vary the length of your Sendaways so that the dog does not get a preconceived idea as to the distance required.

Redirection

'Redirection' is commanding the dog by word, signal, or both to move laterally to the right or left of the position he has arrived at after the original Sendaway outrun; this is a prerequisite at certain levels in Working Trials.

In Obedience, it may be used to correct a poorly directioned Sendaway, but the benefits of this will be very limited. A deviation mark of say eight points may be halved to four with one cleanly executed command, but that extra command itself is likely to carry a penalty of perhaps two points, so the saving achieved will be very nominal and as a result is unlikely to provide sufficient recovery for any significant success.

If you have an interest in combining Obedience and Working Trials, you may wish to teach Redirection, and if so you will no doubt receive good instruction on how to do so from the many books on Working Trials or from advice from your fellow competitors therein. As we only compete with our dogs in Obedience and as explained above Redirection brings very little benefit, in line with our general philosophy of keeping things simple and not cluttering up the dog's brain with unnecessary information, this is one thing we do not teach. The choice is yours.

CHAPTER 10

Advanced Positions on the Move

Attentive flowing Heelwork is an essential ingredient for success in Obedience today. Most minor inaccuracies can recur from time to time, however well you may have trained your dog, but they can be ironed out quickly by returning to basics in Novice work. A dog that has the tendency to hesitate, lag or even stop in Heelwork, however, can be frustrating, even heartbreaking to work. A major contributing factor in creating this type of fault can be the introduction of the Advanced Stand, Sit, and Down on the move, particularly if it is introduced too early in your training programme. It is absolutely vital that you have established completely attentive consistent Heelwork at all paces before you even think about the A.S.S.D. aspect of the exercise.

If the Advanced Positions are not taught methodically, sympathetically, and at the correct time, the rest of your Heelwork will deteriorate, possibly irrevocably. If we recap on what is required it is easy to see why. If trained correctly, your dog has by now learned to stick to you like glue through all manner of twists, turns and changes of pace, but now you require something else. On just a single command or signal he must stop – and stop dead – in any of the three positions. This is much too confusing for a young dog still coming to terms with all the other complexities of Heelwork. Then, on being collected by the handler, he is expected to resume Heelwork in exactly the correct position as though nothing had happened, and of course, like all other aspects of Obedience, it is not just a question of simply getting the correct positions. There are a host of minor inaccuracies which will incur penalty deductions and have to be trained against.

Apart from actually missing a position completely, the dog will also be penalized proportionately for executing the position too slowly, not holding the position solidly until the pick-up (i.e. slight paddle in the stand – moving one leg or more or moving round to watch the handler), anticipating the pick-up when the dog recommences Heelwork with the handler, or not picking up cleanly on command, hesitating or lagging.

The handler can also throw away marks by subconsciously giving extra commands or signals, such as hesitating while the dog responds, excessive head movement, and on pick-up giving the command too soon or too late.

The step from Class B to Class C is a big one for both dog and handler, and the introduction of A.S.S.D. is a major factor. Remember, once you have won out of Class B you only have Class C for the rest of the dog's working life, so it is worth while to bide your time. Commence training when the time is right, and teach methodically and without pressure.

Let us now examine how the A.S.S.D. positions are communicated by the judge, via the steward, to the handler during the test.

The Exercise

The three positions are all required to be carried out in the same predetermined order and point in the Heelwork for each competitor. On approaching the prescribed point in the Heelwork, the steward will inform the competitor that the position is being approached, i.e. 'Position coming'.

The actual position will be communicated to the handler in one of three ways. The handler may be given a card at the commencement of the Heelwork with the positions printed in order. In this case, having warned the handler, the position will be required to be executed as the steward says 'Now' or the position number 'One', 'Two', or 'Three'. (If this method is used beware of excessive head or hand movements as you glance at the card.) Alternatively, the positions may be displayed on small notices positioned at the side of the ring along the Heelwork route, and the handler will be warned and instructed in the same way. Lastly, the positions may be included in the steward's commands, i.e. 'The Sit position is coming'. 'Now'.

Teaching the Exercise

When you feel that you have your dog's confidence in Class B Heelwork and that you are on the verge perhaps of winning, then you have to begin to think seriously about Class C and of course the A.S.S.D. Now is the time and not before, but you should have in your favour a long-established programme of Distance Control training which can now be turned to your advantage.

Although all Class B and C Heelwork is carried out lead free, we begin our introduction to the Advanced Positions back on the lead, and although the positions are only given at normal pace in the ring, we begin by teaching at slow pace.

Advanced Positions – The Sit

Give the command 'Sit' while applying aids used in Distance Control.

Move away from the dog, using the lead to maintain his Sit position.

The Sit

We also teach one position at a time, ensuring that each is consolidated completely before moving to the next. We begin with the Sit. Your dog has become so used to sitting as you come to a Halt that this position, with you proceeding forward without him seems to be the most difficult to come to terms with.

Begin at slow pace on the lead. When you are ready, give your Sit command clearly and positively (you may of course if you wish precede the command with your dog's name but if you do, make sure you use the correct tone of voice as in Distance Control. Having given the command, apply your Sit aid in a similar fashion to Distance Control, that is with the end of

your lead in your right hand passing over your left which can provide upward and backward restraint. Hesitate a little in your forward progress, turning slightly on your left foot and placing your right gently up to your dog's toes before progressing one pace forward. You do not have to leave your dog farther than the lead's length, so that you can maintain the upward and backward restraint as you turn and walk back past him. Turn again, and return to the Heel position.

To avoid the dog anticipating the pick-up, that is to say starting forward before the handler's left leg is exactly level with the dog's shoulder, we always stop in training and praise quietly on the spot before proceeding.

The next step, still at slow pace, is to give

Return past and around the dog to resume the Heel position.

Halt for a few moments before giving the command 'Heel' and proceeding forward with the dog.

the command but without turning, just using the backward tension on the lead. It is important to ensure that the dog responds immediately and if not you must go back to the first step. When your dog will respond to the command with just a light application of the lead, still at slow pace, it is time to try the command alone. Do not forget, take only one pace onward, walk round, and halt by your dog.

Now it is time to go lead free, but maintain your slow pace until you have the position firmly established on one command only. Eventually, your pace can gradually be increased to normal, and the distance you leave between you and your dog can be increased.

With one of the three 'Ts' in mind – Tone of voice – we have noticed on several occasions handlers saying the command very quickly in an attempt to achieve a fast reaction from the dog, so quickly that the word 'Sit' does not have time to register in the dog's brain. He has heard something, but he is not sure what, with the result that he simply stops in his tracks usually still in the Stand. Try to allow the same length of time to say 'Sit' as it takes to say either 'Stand' or 'Down'. You must take care of course not to extend the command too much, but it is worth while making the effort to control your voice in such a way as to give your dog every chance of hearing and understanding. Try saying 'Siit'.

The Down

The Down is the next position to teach. You should have your dog on the lead, and go back to slow pace. If your dog has become used to responding to a good strong 'Down' command without thinking he is being corrected or chastised, there is a very good chance that he will respond to the command without any aid at all. However, if you let the lead loop downward near the ground, as in Distance Control, it will be easy (if necessary) to apply the 'foot on lead' aid while barely breaking pace. Soon the dog will respond to the 'Down' command without aid but still at slow pace and on the lead.

Advanced Positions – The Down

Give the command 'Down', applying again aids used in Distance Control.

Again, after circling your dog, when you return to the Heel position, praise and break off. The lead can now be removed and your pace gradually increased to normal.

The Stand

When the Sit and the Down are firmly established you can turn your attention to the Stand. Once again, revert to slow pace on the lead. As in Distance Control the dog's name in a bright tone precedes this command and the Stand aid (left foot in front of the dog's hind paws combined with light backward restraint from the lead) can be smoothly incorporated in

Move around your dog. At the early stages of teaching this exercise, you may need to use additional commands here.

Return to the pick-up point. Halt for a few seconds before giving the command 'Heel' and proceeding forward with the dog.

your slow pace. As this position is the most precarious to maintain, the aid must be applied for a more prolonged period, and its abandonment will need to be very gradual. Only when the dog will respond to the command alone should be lead be taken off and your pace gradually increased to normal. Although the Stand is perhaps the most time-consuming to teach, once established in the dog's mind it often becomes the most reliable of the three.

The transition to the dog responding to the command while the handler proceeds forward can also be eased by the use of a plank or board similar to that mentioned for the Stand-stay (*see* pp. 38–9).

You can use what we call a 'kick-over' board. Set up a 8–12in (20–30cm) plank against a couple of pegs so that it leans slightly towards you. In Heelwork with your dog, walk toward the board, so that you can pass it but your dog can not. Give your position command just as your dog reaches the board, proceed without your dog, About-turn past your dog, About-turn again, and as you draw level with your dog, tap the board over flat with your foot. Give your 'Heel' command, and proceed forward so that your dog can jump over the flattened board and progress with you. As with the Stays, the height of the board can be reduced until it is non-existent.

Advanced Positions – The Stand

Using the dog's name, give the command 'Stand'. At the same time, use your left foot to apply gentle upward pressure to the dog's belly and exert backward restraint on the lead to encourage a smooth transition from Down to Stand.

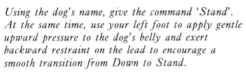

Walk around the dog, using additional commands if necessary to maintain his position.

Return to the pick-up point, halting for a few moments before giving the command 'Heel'. Anticipation is a common fault on this one, so if necessary give the command 'Wait' until you are ready to proceed forward with 'Heel'.

As the exercise becomes more firmly established in the dog's mind, he will develop the tendency to anticipate a position, any position, on the steward's command 'Now', which is used most frequently in the ring. This is why, when we are judging, we instruct our stewards

Stand position, using kick-over board.

The pick-up. Kick the board flat . . .

. . . and proceed forward together.

to say 'Position coming' 'one', etc., as we believe that this creates less anticipation.

The answer is, of course, not always to give your dog a position command, in training, on hearing the 'Now', but to put in a quick 'Heel' or 'Watch Me' command and proceed together.

If you are patient and thorough, by following the foregoing programme, your dog will become confident in this very demanding part of the Heelwork exercise. Remember, though, the consistency of your dog's reaction to the commands hinges almost entirely on the consistency of your tone of voice and clarity of the vowel sounds. Even the best of dogs will inevitably miss a position from time to time, and this will nearly always be attributable to a poor command from the handler. If you correct or even chastise your dog for a missed position, you risk undoing months of hard work.

A missed position in the ring will already be too costly, and correction will achieve little or nothing in terms of salvaging any marks. The apprehension that will be created will be very difficult to overcome, so shrug off the disappointment, and concentrate on establishing what you did to allow things to go wrong and how you can improve your training – in particular your tone of voice – to ensure that the dog gets a clearer message in future.

Basics to Remember

- Train each position separately until perfect.
- Teach at slow pace and on the lead to begin with.
- In training, only rarely pick up on the move. Mostly, come to a Halt before picking up. Occasionally, give a 'Wait' command and proceed past your dog without picking up.
- Don't always give a position on the 'Now' in training, but continue, with encouragement, together.
- Missed positions in competition should be ignored. Correction in the ring will achieve little and is likely to set up apprehension.
- In training, break up your A.S.S.D. positions with some fun, relaxed, fast-pace exercises.

CHAPTER 11

Choosing a Puppy for Obedience

This chapter may appear to come rather late on in our book, but its place is more appropriate than it might seem. Most people already have a dog when they discover our sport and it may be some time before a new addition is considered. The foregoing chapters are, of course, structured around the training of a young dog, but they can equally be applied if your introduction to Obedience comes when your dog is more mature.

Once you have been bitten by the Obedience bug, however, your next dog may well be obtained with Obedience specifically in mind. Never lose sight of the fact, though, that your dog should be, first and foremost, your pet and your friend.

Many people have their own particular favourite breed, often that with which they started, and they remain loyal to that breed whatever the degree of ability or suitability it might exhibit as far as Obedience is concerned. There are, indeed, very few dogs that will not respond to the training methods we have been outlining in the foregoing chapters, and over the years we have seen many examples of unusual breeds competing at quite a high level.

We have seen a Yorkshire Terrier, a Staffordshire Bull Terrier, and a Miniature Poodle taking part in the Crufts Obedience Championships, and recently, since the introduction of the Inter-regional Competition, breeds varying from Corgis to Great Danes have made an appearance. There are certain breeds, however, whose size or conformation, or both, leave the odds of top success in Obedience stacked heavily against them. The dedication and hard work required to get to the top with one of the more suitable breeds can all be used up just keeping your head above water, and the people who choose, stick with, persevere and love their breed, no matter what, have our undying respect.

There is no doubt that the predominantly successful breed in English Obedience is the Border Collie together with its identical non-Breed-Show counterpart, the Working Sheepdog. That is not to say that the acquisition of a Border Collie is an automatic passport to success. We have heard the breed referred to as 'clockwork dogs'. 'Yes', we say 'but you still have to know where to put the key, and which way to wind it'. This also applies to many other breeds of dog. As long as a particular breed is generally agile and reasonably intelligent, there is no reason why it should not be trained right up to top level.

Apart from the Border Collie and the traditional patriarch of Obedience, the German Shepherd Dog, there are many other established and emerging breeds proving themselves in our sport: Golden Retrievers, Labradors, Belgian Shepherd Dogs (Tervs in particular), Dobermans, Shelties, Poodles, and of course many other cross-breeds are currently all well represented and respected.

More important than theoretical intelligence in any breed is sound temperament and a willingness to please, and these are the qualities you should look for in parents and, even more important, grandparents.

Once you have decided to acquire a new pup, do not be rushed into making any rash decisions. Once you have chosen your breed, enquire in the Obedience Show scene about prospective matings from Obedience working stock. Proven working ability in other forms of canine competition is not always a guarantee of success. For instance, progeny from predominantly sheep-oriented Border Collies often prove too strong or independent for Obedience as can some of the gundogs. If you can locate an established Obedience line in a prospective mating for your chosen breed, and you are able to book a puppy provisionally, make sure that you are able to have a look at mum, dad, grandma, and grandpa too, if possible.

A carefully planned mating by a responsible breeder should include positive research down the parents' lines against hereditary defects such as hip dysplasia, progressive retinal atrophy, hereditary cataract, and other particular breed problems. Nothing can be guaranteed, but the odds against can be improved dramatically with careful research and planning. It can be heartbreaking to set out with your youngster on a carefully planned training programme only to find that all your efforts count for nothing as some wretched hereditary disablement begins to manifest itself.

When the pups are born, or if you are informed of a litter which you believe suits your needs, and you go to see them, there are all sorts of theories and tests which have been devised to enable you to make the right choice. 'Don't take the meekie mildie'. 'Avoid the obvious boss dog'. 'Throw an empty match box and take the first one to pick it up'. These and many more old wives' tales or more scientific selection processes exist to help you decide.

In our experience, the most important thing is that you should really deeply *want* your puppy; if he has been planned for, waited for, and at last here he is, something inside will tell you the one for you. If you find yourself looking at a puppy or a litter of puppies and being persuaded, or find that you are trying to persuade yourself that you like this one or that one, it is time to stand back and think again.

All the dogs we have owned that we have been successful with have all been wanted, planned for, and eagerly anticipated. The dogs with which we have not enjoyed so much success have all, on reflection, been acquired on a more calculated basis: the breeding looked right, it was time to start a new youngster, etc. These were not sufficient reasons. That is not to say we have not done our best for them. We have a fourteen-year-old 'no hoper' asleep at our feet as we write this chapter, but the special relationship necessary for top success only developed for us when the selection process centred as much around the heart as around the head.

There is one thing you might try. If you like the look and 'feel' of a puppy, and you hold him up in front of you, and he looks you straight in the eye for a few seconds without looking to left or right, you may well be on the right track. One thing is for sure in our opinion: a genuine desire for one another's company is more important than breed, breeding or pedigree.

CHAPTER 12

At the Show

All your hard work and dedication to training at home and at the club will come to nothing if you don't get things right on show day. Dogs are not machines, and we should not expect them to be. It is the minor mistakes that you make or your fellow competitors make that influence the final result. Anything that you can do to help your dog and yourself feel comfortable and at ease will contribute to the saving of the odd mark here and there which can make all the difference.

Preparation

Setting out and arriving at the show in plenty of time is the first rather obvious move; if you have ever arrived late and rushed into the ring to work you will realize just how disastrous this can be.

If you have arrived in plenty of time, you may be able to pick a shady spot to park the car. On the other hand, at many shows you will find a parking marshall directing you to a space. This can be a thankless task, and you can make it even harder by arguing about where you wish to park. In the end your own peace of mind will also suffer. You should have in your car an old sheet or two as a cover to provide shade from the sun anyway. There are many excellent types of dog guard, rack or cage which you can have fitted so that you can leave your car doors and windows open while your dog is still secure.

Once parked and settled in, the next item on the agenda is to ensure that your dog is exercised and comfortable, especially if your journey has been a long one. Most show societies set aside an exercise area with facilities to collect and deposit your dog's natural bodily functions. It is vital that we all help to keep our show venues clean. They are difficult to come by, and we must all act responsibly and clean up after our dogs. Keep a supply of plastic bags with you to help.

Having settled your dog in, your next move should be to find your rings and 'book in'. Even if you have not received a 'running order' it is worth checking the scoreboard to ensure that you have not been 'drawn'. Running orders do sometimes go astray. If there is any discrepancy or dispute in this area the Chief Steward can be called upon to adjudicate. At the same time as booking in, check and make a note of your Stays time, and establish where the Stay ring is located.

If for any reason you are late arriving at your show, that is to say one hour or so after judging has commenced, you will be unable to book in. Again, the Chief Steward is the official who should be approached regarding your eligibility to work or not.

When you book in, you may be required to choose when you wish to work by putting your ring number down in an appropriate place on the scoreboard or on a separate list. Having done so, you should check the progress of the class regularly so as to ensure that you are ready to work your dog at the appropriate time. You now have a little time to prepare yourself and your dog for your work in the ring.

Ringside

Do not spend too much time around the ring

with your dog, although it is important that he does get acclimatized to the atmosphere. It is worth while watching a round or two to absorb the salient features, but do not try to memorize the whole round. Concentrate on the more advanced classes: Classes B and C. Any of the more intricate turns are worth trying to make a mental note of.

As we mentioned in the Introduction, as you advance through the classes, you will accumulate various Retrieve articles. If you have by now graduated to Class B or C, check the Retrieve article of the day, and try to sort out one from your collection that is similar to practise with. It is surprising how much one can improvise to simulate what is required.

Similarly, one can usually improvise a similar Sendaway to that in the Class B or C ring to practise, but be careful where you do it. If you are too near the ring, you may do more harm than good by giving your dog the wrong preconceived idea where he must go. Also, if you are too closely oriented to the Sendaway markers in the ring you will be accused by your fellow competitors of cheating (and quite rightly so). Practise a Sendaway by all means, and set it up in the same direction in relation to the sun as the one you will be doing in the ring, but make sure you are well away from any situation which causes any distraction to, or takes advantage of, your fellow competitors. Do not forget to call your dog through the markers first.

Just before you are due to go into the ring, a short session of Heelwork just to put your dog on his toes is a good idea, but don't overdo it unless your dog is a workaholic – a few are.

In the Ring

Eventually come those few brief minutes in the ring when all your efforts are put to the test. Almost everyone suffers to some degree from nerves and this in turn transmits to the dog who translates them into a certain amount of apprehension. We have a saying – 'They are all Obedience Champions in the back garden!' The main reason that your dog loses that finely tuned sharpness that you have achieved in training is the additional pressure that you feel in the competitive environment. Your dog is prepared to place himself entirely in your hands in training because he perceives that you are completely in control; when he looks up at you in the ring and gets those 'vibes' of uncertainty, he suddenly realizes that you are not perhaps quite as invincible as you have led him to believe. Thus, he tends to begin to think for himself.

What can you do to lessen the nerves factor? Just realizing that you are not alone in suffering from nerves can be a great help. Almost all the top handlers still get nervous. Indeed, we would suggest that the day you don't feel the old 'butterflies in the tummy' just before you go into the ring is the day to pack it all in.

People deal with their nerves in many ways: deep breathing, joking with their fellow competitors, even yoga, or a quick trip to the bar (but don't overdo it), but the main thing to remember is that there is always next week. We are very lucky in the UK where we can, relatively easily, get to forty, fifty, or more shows in a year. If you can develop the habit of regarding each show as a preparatory work out for the next week, some of those nerves will disappear.

Another thing to remember is our advice regarding your timing in reaction to stewards' commands. It is vital that you do not allow yourself to become intimidated by the steward; he is only human after all!

When you have completed your round, always remember to thank the judge and steward for their time. It is a long day for very little reward. Some judges will be prepared to offer you a critique of your round and an explanation of where your marks were lost; others prefer not to, particularly if time is short. On the other hand, some competitors like to receive a run-down on the round while others prefer to leave the ring as soon as possible.

We believe that the exchange between judge

and handler after the round should be as brief as possible, if at all. We are all different – some more receptive to criticism/praise when the adrenalin is flowing, others wishing to be away as quickly as possible to think things over quietly by themselves. Some judges find it easier to communicate than others.

There is nothing more frustrating as a competitor than to have worked your dog and yourself up to just the right key and then have to wait and wait while the judge gives the previous competitor a resume of the round and a brief training lesson. When judging, we never offer an opinion unless directly asked, and when competing we prefer to leave the ring courteously but quickly. If we have any serious queries, we may approach the judge politely after the class has finished, and when we are judging we are quite prepared to discuss anything with any competitor later.

There are, of course, procedures for making objections if you think there has been a breach of the rules. In this case, the Chief Steward should be consulted.

The Stays

There are a few simple points that require consideration before the Stays. Make sure you are at the Stays ring in plenty of time so that, unless your place is predetermined, you can find yourself the most suitable position. Try to avoid leaving your dog in the Sit facing the sun. The temptation will be for him to close his eyes against the glare which could result in him dozing off and going Down. Try to avoid positioning yourself in the corner of the ring. When you leave your dog for an in-sight Stay you may become hidden by your fellow competitors coming from left and right.

If your dog is to be left in the Down on a spot which has just been vacated by another dog, a certain amount of sniffing can be expected, if you rub your hand thoroughly over the area your familiar scent may be sufficient to eliminate this.

If your dog should move, never return to him and correct or chastise him while the Stays are still in progress. The dog next to you is very likely to take the blame and move, and this will certainly not endear you to your fellow competitors.

Finally, when you have returned to your dog, and the exercise is finished, remember to praise your dog, quietly, in the position he has just completed. Don't release your dog and praise loudly. A ring full of barking dogs and cheering people is not conducive to the best work for someone is an adjacent ring. (It could happen to you one day.) Also, before you leave the ring, check with your steward to ensure that everything has gone smoothly. There have been many instances where dogs have moved marginally without their handlers being aware of it and marks were deducted without the handler knowing why.

Do not forget to check your dog regularly throughout the day to ensure that he is comfortable, exercised, and watered. If you do have to leave him tied up, ensure that he is in no one's way and that he is secure. It is preferable to use a benching chain, as an ordinary lead can easily be chewed through, and above all never tie a dog to anything movable. If you have ever seen a panic-stricken dog flying across a show ground hotly pursued by a chair attached to the other end of his lead, you will understand what we are saying.

Day's End

Having worked your class/es and completed Stays, your day begins to draw to its conclusion. You and your dog may have worked a good round between you and find yourselves with the chance of an award (prizes usually go to the first six). You should make sure that you are available at the ring if you are required for a 'run-off'. It really is a hard day's work when you are judging, and missing competitors are the last thing you want at close of play.

The same thing applies to Scent which takes

place at the end of the class. If you intend to complete this exercise, make sure you are at the ringside when required. If you do not intend to do Scent, the judge will appreciate being informed.

At the end of the day, you may have won or been placed or you may finish nowhere. We keep a diary for all our dogs where we record every round at every show so that we can analyse what went right and what went wrong, and we recommend that you keep one. It can be both a training aid and a morale booster.

Do not forget, when you are on your way home, if you have a rosette, you can look at your dog and say, 'Today *we* got it right', but if things haven't gone so well you must be able to say to yourself, 'Today *I* got it wrong. What can *I* do to put it right?'

As we come to the end of our day at the show, we also come to the end of our book.

We hope that this book has been able to convey some of the excitement, technique, and attraction of our sport. We also hope that it will stimulate you to greater efforts, but we would like to offer you this analogy. Competitive Obedience is like climbing a mountain. When you set out, your aim is to reach the top. Indeed, for many of us, if we did not believe in getting to the top, we would not even begin. However, if one day you look up to the summit and realize that you are not going to make it, turn and look down. The sight that greets you will warm your heart for the view will still be far more rewarding than if you had stayed in the valley below.

Winning may be important, but it is not the winning itself but the special bond that forms as you and your dog get to know each other's every thought that brings the greatest reward. They are not with us for very long at best; make sure you appreciate every minute of it.

Useful Addresses

The Kennel Club
1–5 Clarges Street
Piccadilly
London W1Y 8AB

British Institute of Professional
  Dog Trainers
Bowstone Gate
Disley
Cheshire SK12 2AN

Dog Training Weekly
4/5 Feidr Castell Business Park
Fishguard
Dyfed

Obedience Competitor
Long Meadows
Mooredges
Thorne
South Yorkshire DN8 5RY

Dos and Don'ts

Do train your dog regularly – once or even twice a day – but only for short periods (five to ten minutes at most).

Don't overtrain with single, long boring sessions once or twice a week.

Do train your weakest exercise first, especially first thing in the morning when your dog is pleased to see you.

Don't finish a training session on a sour note. Finish with one of the dog's strongest exercises, so that you both feel confident and satisfied.

Do maintain all your Novice aids and commands when training even your experienced Class C dog.

Don't train by default. If mistakes happen, try to resist the urge to correct your dog; instead go back to first principles, and start again.

Do mix your training in as part of your daily exercise and fun with your dog.

Don't train your dog if you are in a bad mood, if you have had an argument with your wife/husband, or if you feel slightly unwell. It would be better just to take your dog on a pleasant relaxing walk.

Do always use your dog's name (once only in a bright commanding tone), in training, in Retrieve and Scent immediately the dog has picked up the article.

Don't say any more until your dog has completed the Present. Then your praise will be fully appreciated.

Do adopt your Novice Recall position as your dog leaves you on Retrieve and Scent.

Don't waste it by standing in that position before you want your dog to return to the Present position.

Do be self-critical. Keep a daily diary of your training progress, and try to analyse what you are doing right and wrong. Also, keep a show diary.

Don't blame your dog or the judge or your fellow competitors when things go wrong.

Do remember to break your exercises down into simple parts.

Don't Finish your dog after a good Retrieve or Scent Present in training. Break the exercise, and praise.

Do work hard on your timing of commands before you turn.

Don't waste time by using your dog's name in front of your turn commands.

Do start your Distance Control training early.

Don't begin your Advanced Positions in Heelwork until you need them.

Do concentrate on footwork and deportment.

Don't bend over on turns, and especially don't bend over your dog on Presents.

Do always call your dog through the Sendaway before sending in training.

Don't send your dog up to a fence or hedge. Always ensure plenty of space behind the markers in training.

Do train your dogs separately.

Don't train one dog in front of another.

Do praise your dog genuinely. This does not necessarily mean loudly.

Don't allow your praise or the dog's excitement to get out of hand at the end of Stays.

Do learn to look upon your lead as a fine tool.

Don't use it like a sledge-hammer.

Do use titbits, but only sparingly; your voice is the best reward.

Don't work your dog on a full stomach – his or yours.

Do always be prepared to look, listen, and learn from others.

Don't change for change's sake. If what you are doing works, stick to it.

Do train with determination and dedication.

Don't let that determination become obsession. Enjoy your dog.

Glossary

Anticipated Pick-Up   Fault – in Advanced Positions on the move. The dog commences to move forward before the handler arrives at the dog's shoulder and gives the pick-up command.

Anticipation   Fault. The dog anticipates the next section of an exercise before receiving the command from the handler, i.e. the dog comes before being called on Recall or sets off for the Retrieve article before being sent.

Backward Present   Fault. The space between the dog and the handler in the Present is considered by the judge as too great. (This is a matter of individual judgement rather than a specific dimensional requirement.)

Backward Work – Lagging   Fault. The dog appears to lack enthusiasm or confidence and hangs behind the required position. In fast pace this fault can deteriorate into a distinct gap between dog and handler or even culminate in the dog stopping completely.

Blank   Article or cloth in Scent pattern uncontaminated by human scent.

Catalogue   The club or society organizing a show are required to publish a list of competitors allocated to their various classes, their running order where applicable, and any other relevant information, such as Stays times, notice of reserve judges, etc.

Contact Present   Fault. The dog is considered to be at fault by some (not all) judges if he is too close to the handler, i.e. making physical contact. More commonly, the dog will be penalized if he approaches too fast and bumps into the handler's legs as he sits.

Crabbing   Fault. A term applied during Heelwork when the track of the dog's hind legs falls perceptibly outside the track of the front legs. This fault is usually exhibited when the track of the dog's hind legs is much further away from the handler than the front, but occasionally it can occur if the dog 'tucks in' too much so that the track of his hind legs falls inside that of the front relative to the handler.

Creep   Fault in the Down position on the move, or the Down-stay. Although the dog holds the position, he may 'creep' slightly forward without actually showing daylight underneath.

Crooked Present   Fault. The dog's spine is perceptibly not square, i.e. to the line of the handler's feet and shoulders.

Crooked Sit   Fault. The dog's spine is perceptibly at an angle less than or more than 90 degrees to the line of the handler's shoulders and feet.

Croup (Early) Pick-Up   Fault in Advanced Positions on the move. The handler gives the pick-up command too early, i.e. at the dog's hind quarters rather than at the shoulder.

Decoy   Article or cloth scented by appointed person other than handler or judge – to be rejected by dog.

Dip   Fault. The dog anticipates a Halt, usually due to a lack of continuity in the handler's deportment, and half-Sits.

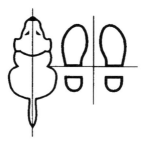
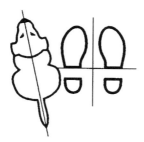

Sit at heel   Crooked   Crooked

Entry Form The details of the dog's name, sex, and breeding, together with the allocation of classes to be entered are set out on a pro forma, together with the entrant's name and address, and returned with the appropriate entrance fee by the prescribed date to the show secretary.

Extra Command (Signal) Fault. An additional signal (or signals) over and above those allowed, is/are given in order to complete an exercise. The signal may have been given because the dog obviously failed to respond or as an additional aid to help a young or inexperienced dog to complete an exercise. Extra signal commands are more prevalent than the verbal version. A subconscious shoulder movement or nod of the head will help to guide your dog in a certain direction. This should and will be interpreted by the judge as an extra command and penalized accordingly.

Extra Command (Verbal) Fault. An additional verbal command or commands over and above that which is permitted within the rules for a particular exercise in a particular class. Extra commands generally fall into three categories: 1) the dog obviously fails to respond to the initial command and requires a further command or commands to comply; 2) the handler gives an extra command knowingly in order to help a young inexperienced dog, being fully prepared to sacrifice some penalty points; 3) the handler gives an involuntary extra command.

Forward or Backward Sit (at Heel) Fault. The line of the dog's shoulder is perceptibly forward of or behind the handler's leg.

Forward Work Fault. The dog appears to 'take over', moving forward of the required position. The enthusiasm for work which creates the fault is admirable, but it is nevertheless a fault.

Heelwork Position While moving forward together in Heelwork, the dog must maintain a constant position relative to the handler. The dog's shoulder should remain sensibly level with the handler's left leg, and the space between the dog and handler should remain nominal (light contact is generally regarded as acceptable).

Hesitation Fault. The dog loses position by dropping back momentarily as the handler steps out from a turn.

Impeding Fault. Often, though not always, associated with crabbing. During Heelwork the dog's position is too close to the handler. Physical contact, otherwise known as 'laying on' makes it difficult for the handler to walk naturally.

Judge The official appointed by the society to judge a particular and specific class.

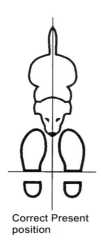

Correct Present
position

Crooked Present

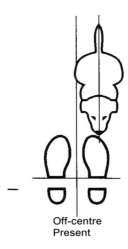

Off-centre
Present

Knee   Fault. The dog makes brief contact with the handler's left leg – usually on a Left Turn.

Off-Centre Present   Fault. The dog's spine is perceptibly more in line with one or other of the handler's feet rather than central.

Overshoot   Fault. On a Halt during Heelwork the dog may overshoot or continue forward slightly before returning to the Sit position.

Paddle   Fault in the Stand position on the move or the Stand-stay. Although holding the position, the dog may take one small pace or two forward.

Pick-Up   Apart from the pick-up of the Retrieve or Scent article by the dog, the term also refers to the point in A.S.S.D. when the handler rejoins the dog and they proceed forward again together.

Present Position   The dog at the Sit in front of, and facing, the handler. The dog should be 'straight', that is the line of the dog's spine should be straight and square to the line of the handler's feet and shoulders. Applies to return in Novice Recall, Retrieve at all levels, and Scent at all levels.

Reserve Judge   In the event of over sixty entries received for any scheduled class (except Ch.C), the person appointed by the society in accordance with Kennel Club Rules to judge the remaining entries. (The number of entries is split equally at random.)

Ring   The area set aside and demarked wherein a particular test is judged.

Ring Steward   The person appointed to call out the judge's instructions to the competitors, i.e. the Heelwork route, or the various commands in Recalls, Retrieve, Scent, etc. A judge may not take on those responsibilities himself.

Run-Off   If, on completion of the whole class, the allocated places can not be decided because two or more dogs are on the same mark, they will be required to 'run-off' by completing one or more of the scheduled exercises again.

Scent Article/Cloth   Article or cloth scented by handler or judge – to be identified by the dog and retrieved.

Scent Pattern   The layout of the Scent articles, i.e. straight line, a 'V' shape, circle, etc.

Schedule   The club or society organizing a show are required to publish a schedule of the classes available for entry, the judges appointed to officiate, and a list of the organizing officials. Within the schedule is an entry form. Schedules are available from show secretaries whose addresses are printed in the *Kennel Gazette* and the two recognized Obedience dog training publications – *Dog Training Weekly* and *Obedience Competitor* – and are often handed out at earlier shows.

Scoreboard Steward   The person appointed to record the scores, or points deducted, on a ringside scoreboard, at the end of each round so that these scores are available for inspection by the other competitors in that class.

Scribe   Some judges, particularly in the advanced classes, appoint an additional steward to whom they can communicate their marks for recording so that they can maintain a more consistent observation of the competitor and dog.

Setting Up   The preparation of the dog in the ring prior to the commencement of the judged part of an exercise, i.e. in Sendaway prior to standing up straight clear of your dog to await the Send instruction from the steward, the procedure of pointing the dog in the right direction and encouraging to 'Look straight' is known as 'setting the dog up'.

Sit Position (at Heel)   The dog in the sit position on the left-hand side of, and facing the same way as, the handler. The dog should be straight, i.e. the spine perceptibly square to the line of the handler's shoulder and feet, parallel to the line of travel. The dog should be close to the handler's leg (no more than an inch or so gap), and the dog's shoulder should be level with the handler's leg. Applies on commencement of all exercises, in Halts during Heelwork and the end of Class A Recall, Recall from Sendaway and in the Finish of Novice Recall, Retrieve at all levels, and Scent at all levels.

Stays Ring   A ring set aside from all others where the Stay exercises for the various tests are carried out. This is to ensure that the dog's position in the Class Test ring does not create any advantage or disadvantage in the execution of the remainder of the test, i.e. Sendaway direction.

Stays Steward (Chief Stays Steward)   The official appointed to observe and report on your dog in the Stays. A Stays steward is usually allocated about six dogs to watch. The Chief Stays Steward is responsible for general organization of the Stays, commencement on time, starting and concluding each Stay in the prescribed time, advising the Stay stewards of time elapsed at points of fault, etc. The class judge is also required to be present during Stays.

Tight Lead   Fault. In Beginners, Novice and Class A half of the heelwork is carried out on the lead, which must remain slack at all times. If it becomes tight, either as a result of the dog going wide or because the handler uses it to maintain the dog's position, it is penalized.

Wides   Fault. In Heelwork the dog deviates perceptibly away from the acceptably correct position relative to the handler's left leg. (Again this is a matter of individual judgement rather than a specific dimensional requirement.) In particular the dog may seem to drift wide as the handler executes a Right or Right About-turn. The term is also registered as a fault if the dog moves too far from the handler while completing the Finish in either direction.

Wide Sit   Fault. The space between the dog and handler is considered to be too great. (This is a matter of individual judgement without any specific dimensional requirement.)

Index

anticipation, 23–4, 69, 70, 73, 95
attention, 17, 24

British Institute of Professional Dog Trainers, 9, 106

class, types of, 10
Class A Recall, 71–3
    slow rejoin, 73
collar, 13–14
Come Fore (Recall), 18, 19, 22
commands
    steward's, 58
    timing, 12, 25, 50, 58–9
    tone of voice, 11–12
    vowel sounds, 13
competition, 9
confidence, 60
crabbing, 24
Crufts Obedience Championship, 6
curiosity, 80

default, training by, 12, 53
deportment, 28, 59
deviation, 24
Distant Control, 29–35
    missed positions, 34
    movement in, 34
distraction, 40, 52
dog's name, use of, 25, 29, 31, 50, 52
dumb-bell, 14–16

enthusiasm, 25
excitement, 25

Finishes, 41–6
foot aids, 29–33
footwear, 15, 59
footwork, 26, 50–8

Halts, 25, 58
Heelwork, 24–8, 47–61
    advanced, 93–9
    changes of pace, 59–60
    forward work, 61
    heel free, 59
    inattention, 60
    lagging, 60–1
Hold, 63

impulsion, 19, 58

Kennel Club, 9, 10, 11, 105

lagging, 60–1
lead, 13–14
Look, 88–9, 90

markers (Sendaway), 84
mat, 89, 90
mouthing, 69
movement,
    in Distant Control, 34
    in Stays, 39–40

nerves, 103

pace, changing, 48, 59
peck, 75
play, 15
playtoy, 24, 61, 76, 77
praise, 12
Presents, 18, 19, 22–3
    crooked, 70
Pykett, Ken, 6

Recall, 17–23
redirection, 92
Retrieve, 62–70
    mark, 65
    mouthing, 69
    overrun, 69
    slow rejoin, 69

Scent Discrimination, 74–82
Seal, John, 6
Sendaway, 65, 83–92
shows, 102–5
    stewards, 58
slow rejoin, 24, 69, 73
Stays, 36–9
    movement in, 39–40

temperament, 11, 39, 100
timing, 12, 25, 50, 58–9
turns, 50–9
    About Turns, 55–7
    Left, 52–5
    Right, 50–1
vocabulary, dog's, 13

Watch, 24, 26
waterproof clothes, 15
Wyant, Charlie, 6